Faith's Fuel

Get Inspired by the Correct Conclusion!

Rudi Louw

All Scripture quotations not taken from the RSV, NKJV, or Mirror Study Bible are my own literal translation or Paraphrase translation of the Scriptures.

The Holy Scriptures are just that, HOLY.

Statements enclosed in brackets were inserted into Scripture quotations to add emphasis or clarify the meaning of what is being said in those scriptures. The integrity of God's Word to Man was not compromised in any way. Due care and diligence was cautiously exercised to keep the Word of Truth intact.

For example: The apostle Paul said in his letter to Timothy in 2 Timothy 3:16 that, *"All Scripture is given by inspiration of God* (literally God breathed)*, and is profitable for doctrine, for reproof, for correction, for instruction **in righteousness**,"* NKJV

Contents

The Marvel of the Holy Bible

1. Uninterrupted Theme and Inspired Thought

It took *1,500 years* to compile the Holy Bible, involving *more than 40 different authors.* <u>Yet</u> the theme and inspired thought of Scripture continues *uninterrupted* from author to author, from beginning till end.

2. Absence of Mythical Stories

Compare philosophies and theories about creation in the Middle East, Europe, Asia, Africa, and Latin America and you'll find mythical scenarios: gods feuding and cutting up other gods to form the heavens and the earth, etc.

In ancient Greek mythology, the Greeks see Atlas carrying the earth on his shoulders. In India, Hindus believe eight elephants carry the earth on their backs.

But in contrast, Job, the oldest book in the Holy Bible, declares that, *"God suspends the earth on nothing."(Job 26:7)*

This was said millennia before Isaac Newton discovered the invisible laws of gravity that delicately balance every planet and sun in its individual circuit.

Contrary to every other ancient attempt to give a creation account, *the Holy Bible pictures the creation of the earth in a very scientific manner.*

For example, in Genesis Chapter One, the continents are lifted from the seas, then vegetation is formed and later animal life, all reproducing *'according to its own kind',* **thus recognizing the fixed genetic laws.** In addition, we have the bringing forth of man and woman, *all done by God in a dignified and proper manner, without mythological adornments.*

The balance or remainder of the Holy Bible follows suite.

The narratives are **true historical documents***, faithfully reflecting society and culture* **as history and archaeology would discover them thousands of years later. Not only is the Holy Bible historically accurate, it is also reliable when it deals with scientifically proven subjects.** It was never intended to be a textbook on history, science, mathematics, or medicine. *However, when its writers touch on these subjects,* **they often state facts that scientific advancement would not reveal, or even consider, until thousands of years later.**

While many have doubted the accuracy of the Holy Bible, time and continued research have consistently demonstrated that the Word of God is better informed than its critics.

3. Intactness

Of all the ancient works of substantial size, *the Holy Bible survives intact, against all odds and expectations.*

Compared with other ancient writings, the Holy Bible has more manuscripts as evidence to support it than any ten pieces of classical literature combined!

The plays of William Shakespeare, for instance, were written about four hundred years ago, after the invention of the printing press. Many of his original writings and words have been lost in numerous sections, *yet the Holy Bible's uncanny preservation has weathered thousands of years of wars, contradictions, persecutions, fires and invasions.*

Through the centuries Jewish scribes have preserved the Holy Bible's Old Covenant text, ***such as no other manuscripts have ever been preserved. They kept tabs on every letter, syllable, word and paragraph.*** *They continued from generation to generation to appoint and train special groups of men within their culture* ***whose sole duty it was to***

preserve and transmit these documents <u>with perfect accuracy and fidelity</u>.

Who ever bothered to count the letters, syllables, or words of Plato, Aristotle, or Seneca for that matter?

When it comes to the New Testament, the actual number of preserved manuscripts is so great that it becomes overwhelming. ***There are more than 5,680 Greek manuscripts, more than 10,000 Latin Vulgate manuscripts and at least 9,300 other versions. Further still, there exists an additional 25,000 manuscript copies of portions of the New Testament.*** **No other document of antiquity even begins to approach such numbers.**

The closest in comparison is Homer's <u>Iliad</u>, with only 643 manuscripts. The first complete work of Homer only dates back to the 13th century.

4. Unmatched Accuracy in Predictive Foretelling

The Holy Bible is unmatched in accuracy in predictive foretelling. No other ancient work succeeds in this, or even begins to attempt this.

Other books such as the Koran, the Book of Mormon, and parts of the Veda claim divine inspiration; ***but none of these books contain predictive foretelling.***

8

This one undeniable fact we know for certain: *While microscopic scrutiny would show up the imperfections, blemishes, and defects of any work of Man, <u>it magnifies the beauties and perfection of God</u>. Just as every flower displays in accurate detail the reflection and perfection of beauty, <u>so does the Word of Truth when it is scrutinized</u>.*

Historian Philip Schaff wrote:

"Without money and weapons, Jesus the Christ conquered more millions than Alexander, Caesar, Mohammad, and Napoleon. Without science and learning, He (Jesus the Christ) shed more light on things human and divine than all philosophers and scholars combined. Without the eloquence of schools, He (Jesus the Christ) spoke such words of life as was never spoken before or since and produced effects which lie beyond the reach of orator or poet. Without writing a single line, He (Jesus the Christ) set more pens in motion and furnished themes for more sermons, orations, discussions, learned volumes, works of art, and songs of praise **than the whole army of great men of ancient and modern times combined.***" (The Person of Christ, p33. 1913)*

Today, there are literally billions of Bibles in more than 2,000 languages.

Isn't it about time you find out what it really has to say?

Hey listen, the Holy Bible is all about Jesus, the Messiah, the Christ…

…and everything about Jesus Christ is really about YOU!!

Study Tips:

Read 2 Corinthians 5:14, 16, 18, 19, and 21.

In the light of these Scriptures, it should be obvious that, if you want to study the Holy Bible, *you should study it in the light of Mankind's redemption!*

Feed daily on **redemption realities** found in the book of Acts, in Romans Chapters One through Eight, and in Ephesians, Colossians, and Galatians, also in 1 Peter Chapter One, 2 Peter Chapter One, James Chapter One, as well as in 1 and 2 Corinthians.

Acknowledgments

I want to acknowledge and thank one of my mentors in the faith, Francois du Toit, for blessing and impacting my life with revelation knowledge.

The portion on *"The marvel of the Holy Bible"* was borrowed from his website, http://www.mirrorword.net/, as students so often feel they have a right to do with things that come from teachers they respect. Just as Galatians 6:6 says, *"Let him who is taught the Word **share in all good things** with him who teaches."*

To all our dear friends and family, for all the love and support, and to all those who helped me with this project:

THANK YOU!

Also, especially to my wife, Carmen;

For keeping me genuine by being my companion in life and partner in ministry,

I love and appreciate you so very much!

Foreword

Thank you for taking the time to read this book.

Let me start off by saying that *I am totally addicted to my Daddy's love for me.*

I am in love with Jesus Christ, *and that is enough for me!*

The love of God is so much more than a doctrine, a philosophy, or a theory. It is so much more and goes so much deeper than knowledge; it way surpasses knowledge.

We are talking heart language here.

I write *to impact people's hearts,* to make them see the mysteries that have been hidden in Father God's heart concerning Christ Jesus, and actually *concerning THEM,* so as to arrest their conscience with it, *that I may introduce them to their original design and to their true selves,* **and present them to themselves perfect in Christ Jesus** *and set them apart unto Him in love,* as a chaste virgin.

We are involved with the biggest romance of the ages.

Therefore this book cannot be read as you would a novel: *casually.* It is not a cleverly devised little myth or fable. **It contains** revelation into some things you may or may not have considered before.

It is the TRUTH of God, ultimate TRUTH, and therefore has direct bearing upon YOUR life. **The Word and the Spirit are my witness** *to the reality of these things!*

Be like the people of Berea whom the apostle Paul ministered to in Acts 17:11. Open yourself up to study the revelation contained in this book **to discover for yourself the reality of these things**.

Be forewarned! Do not become guilty of the sins of the Pharisees, **or you too will miss out on the depth of fulfillment God Himself, who is LOVE, wants to give YOU**.

Jesus said of the Pharisees and Sadducees that they strain out every little gnat BUT swallow whole camels. What He meant by that is that *some people seem to have it all together when it comes to doctrine and they love to argue.*

It makes them feel important, but it is nothing other than EMPTY religious and intellectual pride.

They know the Scriptures in and out, and YET they are still so IGNORANT about **REAL TRUTH that is only found in LOVE.**

They are still so ignorant and indifferent **towards the things that REALLY MATTER.**

14

They are always arguing over the use of *every little jot and tittle* and over the meaning and interpretation of *every word of Scripture.*

The exact thing they accuse everyone else of doing though, the precise thing they judge everyone else for, *they are actually doing themselves.* That is **they often downright misinterpret and twist what is being said, *making a big deal of insignificant things while obscuring or weakening God's real truth: the truth of His LOVE*.**

*They are always majoring on minors **<u>because they do not understand the heart of God</u>** and therefore they constantly miss the whole point of the message*.

Paul himself said it so beautifully,

*"…the letter kills but **the Spirit BRINGS LIFE;**"*

*"…<u>knowledge puffs up</u>, but **LOVE EDIFIES**."*

I say again:

Allow yourself to get caught up in the revelation I am about to share.

Open yourself up to study the insight contained in this book, *not only with a desire to gain knowledge, but also with anticipation **to hear from Father God yourself, to encounter Him through His Word, and to embrace truth, in order to know and believe the LOVE God has for <u>you</u>**, so that you may get so caught up* *in it,* ***that you too may receive from Him LOVES' impartation of LIFE.***

This revelation contains within it the voice and call of LOVE Himself to every human being on the face of this earth. *If you take heed to it, and yield yourself fully to it,* ***it is custom designed and guaranteed to forever alter and enrich your life!***

"...designated,
Son of God, **in power,**

according to (or by) the Spirit

of holiness (of Love),

by His resurrection
from the dead,

Jesus Christ our Lord,

through whom we have
received **grace and apostleship,
to bring about**

*the obedience **of** faith*

for the sake of His name

*among **and within** the nations,*

including yourselves,
who are invited
to belong to Jesus Christ
(...in other words,
you too are included in this
and invited into this!)"

- Romans 1:4-6

Prayer

Thank you Father that You have drawn near to us *and that we are no longer worshiping an unknown God!*

Thank you that You have revealed Yourself; *that You have made Yourself known, in Your Son.*

And so, we thank you that as we look into Your Scriptures, *we are not looking into an inferior picture of God, we are not looking into some clumsy attempt of Man to portray the invisible One, but we, by Your Spirit of Truth, are looking into the face of Your own excellence and beauty; that beauty that surpasses knowledge – that excellence that surpasses our definition!*

So Father, we thank You for the Holy Spirit and His focus upon the Truth, upon Jesus; for His unction upon the Word of life, *to so portray Him, to so portray the invisible God made flesh, to so portray Jesus, **that we may see Him, that we may behold Him, that He may become tangibly ours, our full inheritance within an eternal embrace!***

We thank you for the Scriptures! We thank you for what You communicate to our understanding *through the truth of the gospel;*

through the Word of life written about in those
Scriptures!

Father, as I write and interact with these
precious people, *with Your precious children
reading this book,* I thank you that Your
anointing is upon me, from within me, *to
accurately communicate Your Word!*

I thank you that You think Your thoughts
through my thoughts, *and type through my
fingers,* so that our audience, Father, *would be
unaware of the word of Man, but awesomely
aware of the Word of God!*

We worship You Lord.

O how we love Your oracles; *Your Word, Your
LOGOS; Jesus Himself – Your very utterance
in Him!*

How we treasure *that Word **within us!***

**Your words were found, and we ate them,
and they became to us the delight of our
heart!**

Father, thank you for precious lives reading
this book, and perhaps also reading our other
books, and grasping and appreciating our
message to them in it.

*Every life represented carries the value of Your
Son's death, burial, and resurrection; the very
value of Your Son Himself!*

And so, in the light of that, *we esteem one another!*

Father, prepare every reader, every heart, *to partake of this covenant meal set before us; laid out before us in Your redemption truth,* **like a banquet!**

And so, as we partake together Father, *I thank you that we do indeed recognize one another's worth, in Your opinion of us!*

In the revelation of *Your love-plan; that romance of the ages we have been invited into!*

I thank you that we can *extend and impart* our experience of You *to each other.*

Blessed be Your name!

We worship You Lord!

Amen!

Chapter 1

Measure Accurately!

In all the previous 5 books in this Faith Inspired Ministry series, we have studied together around the theme of *our personal, practical application of the Word; of the truth of the Gospel; of redemption realities.* I do believe that these are perhaps some of the most important concepts and teachings *that anyone could ever share with you.* So please, if you have not read the previous 5 books in this series yet, make sure that you get and read them all; or you can now also get the Study Manual which is all 6 books in one.

Every one of these books put into a Study Manual were written to help you come to a clear, accurate understanding *of your contribution, of what God expects you to do **in order to receive all that He has labored for** on your behalf*!

All that He has labored for on your behalf *is your portion*!

Everything that God labored for, for you, all that He accomplished for you, on your behalf, *is exactly what He has in mind for you to appropriate in your heart, and enjoy, and manifest!*

God doesn't have **a lesser value, a lesser measure** of all that He worked for *in mind for any of us!*

The only reason why some of us continue to live in a frustrated experience in our faith *is simply because **we have not yet fully laid a hold of, grasped, and believed** all that He has worked for and accomplished in Christ Jesus!*

God is not to blame if there is prevailing evidence in your spirit and life, in your testimony, *of need and of lack!*

He says, *"I have come that you might have LIFE, and have it more abundantly!"*

And so, *only within the light of what He accomplished* do we find access into that life-quality that Jesus calls, *"abundance".*

That *"abundance"* is our portion, nothing less, amen!

You see, we as a believer's fellowship, our *"Church"* family, the friends we fellowship with; us all together involved in the one ministry of Jesus Christ to this world, my wife and I included, **will not settle for less than His *"abundance."*** And in this book I am going to do my best to inspire you also *to not settle for anything less in your life than His "abundance!"*

Why settle for lack if He's your Shepherd?

If I can say with David the prophet, *in that same confidence, "The Lord is my Shepherd, I shall not want", then surely goodness and mercy shall follow me too,* **all the days of my life!**

Dear friend, *God desires* **that testimony** *to be your daily experience also!*

You see, for a long time, as *"The Church,"* even as Christians, even as believers, *we have limited our testimony to our experience!* We have allowed our experience to become a measure we look at, gauge, and consider, **beyond the measure of the Word!**

Listen, while you still allow your personal experience to be your conversation, *and the measure of your life,* **the revelation of redemption will disappoint you!**

Make His testimony your testimony!

Make His witness of His Son; *make His truth, your testimony!*

Establish in your heart **that what God says concerning you in the light of what He has revealed and accomplished in Christ Jesus is the final testimony of your life!**

Establish in your heart that **it's the absolute truth concerning you!**

The only boundary I will allow to define my life is what God says concerning me! It's *the only thing I will measure my life by!*

You can also establish these things in your own heart! And if you do, let me tell you something, *I can guarantee you that **your experience will follow!***

Praise God!

Hallelujah!

Now, please have your Bible by your side as you read this book and please go with me to Romans Chapter 1. I want to draw your attention to Verse 5. *If you don't have a Bible then don't worry man, just relax and follow along as best you can.*

Chapter 2

We Received Grace and Apostleship *All in One!*

Romans 1:5,

"...through whom (he is referring to Jesus Christ);"

"...through whom we all have received grace..."

You see *everything that Jesus Christ accomplished;* **that grace was released to us!**

Let me say it another way: *In everything that He accomplished* **grace was released to us!**

"...through Him we received grace!" Paul *says,*

"...through what He did..."

"...we received grace; we received that grace of what He accomplished;"

"...and in that grace, we received the grace of God and its influence within our lives;"

"...it is the result of what He accomplished!"

Paul says,

*"…we received grace **and apostleship;"***

Now listen, don't get all tied up in knots over, what religion thinks are titles. Don't get hung up on Paul, *the **Apostle**, and **Prophet** So-and-so, and **Evangelist** So-and-so, and **Pastor** So-and-so, or **Teacher** So-and-so.* Jesus didn't intend for us to be all puffed up in pride *and therefore to end up with no real substance in our hearts,* and then only being left with and stuck with a bunch of big titles and positions!

Listen; He didn't die for us *and then leave us with empty titles and positions to inherit!*

No! He didn't leave us with that!

He said,

"The Gentiles exercise lordship over each other, and those who exercise authority over another is called 'a benefactor'."

*"…BUT NOT SO AMONG YOU. **On the contrary**, he who wants to be the greatest among you, **let him be as the younger; let him be a love-slave to his brothers.** And he who wants to govern, **let him be as one who serves, as one who is nothing but a servant**."*

*"For who is greater, he who sits at the table, **or he who serves?** Is it not he who sits at the*

table? **Yet I am not sitting at the table, but I am among you as one who serves!***" - Luke 22:25-27.

He turned their theories and worldly philosophies *about titles and authority and jockeying for positions in ministry* on its head!

In another translation He says,

*"If you want to be great in God's kingdom, **learn to be the servant of all!***" - Mark 10:43.

He gave us **functions, *not a bunch of titles and positions of authority!*** He gave us **functions!** He gifted us to function, in love!

It is love and passion that motivates and becomes the driving force within us; that *becomes the very driving force behind New Testament ministry and ministers!*

Obtaining empty titles and positions cannot be the driving force behind ministry, amen!

Serving Mammon cannot be the driving force behind what we do in ministry, amen!

Getting into ministry for the money, because of greed, because you have wealth in mind, cannot be the driving force behind ministry!

Simply just getting into ministry because you have a paycheck in mind, and being motivated in what you do by that paycheck, cannot be the driving force behind ministry!

Jesus is not looking for a bunch of hirelings in ministry!

If the motivation of your heart is still caught up in money, authority, and fame, *you are missing it big time in ministry my friend!*

We cannot afford to look at ministry as yet another career opportunity, *as a job!*

I say again: We, because of worldly thinking, have made titles and jobs out of *what God released amongst us to be **functions of service because of love!***

We are servants **to equip the saints.**

Romans 1:5,

*"...through whom we have received grace **and apostleship...**"*

Apostleship is not some office that Paul occupied in terms of the world's understanding of the *"Managing Director"* or the *"Chief Executive Officer"* of some business!

Apostleship was and still is a love-ministry of the laying down of someone's life for someone else! Apostleship is a ministry of such excellence in love that many times your only repute is that of what God thinks about you!

That apostleship, that ministry of passion, of walking in God's love, of walking in a strong uncommon kind of a love, of walking in the same kind of love that was on display in Jesus, *walking in a love that focuses strongly on the truth of the gospel, and what it really has to say to you **about you** and **about others; how forgiven, how freed, how loved we all are**,* will cause you to be misunderstood, many times. It causes you to face ill-repute!

Paul didn't find or use his apostleship as some kind of title he could hide behind, or **some kind of an exalted position that he managed to attain to through his years of experience in religion!**

No! He received his apostleship on the same basis upon which he received God's grace! **He received it as a gift, *and not to him, but to others!***

*...That apostleship came **at the same time** his eyes opened to the truth of the grace of God, and what God accomplished, by that grace, in Christ Jesus!*

In other words: *He received that apostleship, that compelling and commissioning influence of the Love of God upon his heart **at the same time as he received grace!***

As he embraced God's grace, *that apostleship was awakened and birthed within him by that same working of that grace within his heart!*

Let me put it to you this way: **It was within his discovery of that revelation of what God did**

in Christ that that apostleship was birthed within him; *an energy, a motivating force, was released within him!*

You really should also read my book on *Equipped for Ministry,* where I expound **on this birthing** within Paul's heart, and within the believer's heart, for ministry, and then I also go into more detail about it in the book series and Study Manual called: *The Gospel In 3-D!*

I also wrote another book as companion to all these already mentioned called: *Fulfillment In Ministry,* and if you are going to go through these books on ministry I put together, or f you are in ministry already, or feel called to be in the ministry, you really should read that one as well. *It will greatly bless you and help you!*

That word, APOSTELO, used in the original Scriptures means **to be thrust forth, to be sent out, to be compelled to go!**

And so Paul says, *"...my ministry has come all the way to Rome..."*

And you can go and study the maps for yourself *to see and discover* **the fuel,** *in Paul's experience of the revelation of the gospel,* **which took him far beyond the comfort zone** *...which took him far beyond the boundaries of his air-conditioned office in Jerusalem or Damascus for that matter!*

Ha... ha... ha...

If you too discover faith's fuel, you'll discover a new energy, a new fountain, a new resource of life within you *that will take you beyond your own struggles!* It will take you beyond your own job-description! *It will even coax you out of your own comfort zone!*

Ha... ha... ha...

How many people have lived a ruined, robbed life, *by limiting their life to a mere job-description* **just because someone else is prepared to pay their price; to match what the world calls** <u>**value**</u>**!**

They have lived a ruined, robbed life, because they have bought into a lie!

In Christ Jesus grace comes to you, and grace brings new definition to your life!

When Paul says, *"I am what I am by the grace of God,"* **he was not making some excuse for weakness in his life!** No, he was advertising the revelation he carried within his bosom. He was advertising his ministry!

He says in Romans 11:13,

"I magnify my ministry!"

I can just hear it already,

'Hey, you sound so arrogant Paul!'

But you see, he was so confident, so persuaded that he had died, and that the life which he then represented, in that flesh body he lived in, was *the resurrection life and love of Jesus Christ!*

He had become so confident that he had the mind and heart of Christ, *that there was no longer for him any concern for his own reputation, but **one** concern **only**, and **it is for the truth of the gospel; for the truth of Man's redemption, already accomplished by God, in Christ, to be embraced fully!***

He was concerned **for THIS gospel, God's gospel, and its apostleship! He was concerned for it to be so accurately, clearly, simply, and plainly represented to Man** *that we would be left without an excuse to BE all that God calls us in His Word to BE!*

God calls us all *His children!*

And so he speaks there in Romans 1 of an apostleship, a commission that he had received **because of this grace.** And this apostleship, this commission, this motivating passion and driving force **had become the identity of his life!** So he says that his aim, his target in apostleship is this:

*"**To bring about the obedience of <u>faith</u> for the sake of His name** (for the sake of that identification in Jesus) **among** (or within) **all the nations.**"*

34

Verse 6 says,

"...including yourselves;"

"...you also are identified already as belonging to Jesus Christ!"

Our apostleship *is the extension of the heart of God,* **calling the nations to be identified in Christ; to discover themselves associated in Christ already; to recognize their authentic Identity in Him, fully restored to them! God is calling the nations to belong again; because as far as He is concerned, as far as His heart is concerned, they always have belonged!**

They belong to Him and in Him!

Hallelujah!

And so we see that Paul is very clear and very sure in his own understanding of his ministry.

Chapter 3

Seeing faith accurately!

Paul sees *the impact of his ministry* to be that of **so releasing an obedience of <u>faith</u>, a faith of such quality that Man's contribution would no longer be limited and hampered by his own religious efforts!**

Paul sees *the impact of his ministry* to be that of **releasing such accurate faith that Man's contribution would be the inspiration of that faith,** that it would be the inspiration that God's faith in His Son's revelation and labor quickens within them.

Look with me at Romans 1:17. Paul, *speaking of his ministry and of his gospel and of the true gospel for which he is not ashamed,* says,

"...for in it; in this gospel, in the gospel of God, the righteousness of God **is revealed; it's made known. That righteousness is made known, from faith to faith!"**

You see, it's **the revelation of this Gospel, of the gospel of God; it's the revelation** of righteousness, of original true righteousness fully restored, it's **this revelation** that **fuels faith** in the heart of Man!

It's **righteousness, plain and simple;** it's **this revelation, this love, this purity, this innocence** *fully restored to us in Christ in His work of redemption* which **fuels faith** in the heart of Man!

See, *faith* **is not reward inspired!**

Faith is truth inspired! *...And what truth is that?* **The truth of His love!**

So, therefore, faith is love inspired!

Faith has been taught among many Christian circles, very popularly lately, but very inaccurately so, as *something you've got to put out there for a certain reward.*

They say, *'Believe God, come on, use your faith, put your faith out there. Use that substance for better health and wealth!'*

And it all sounds so good, and so spiritual. They say, *'Believe Him! Use the substance of your faith for better vehicles or a better standard of living!'*

But listen now; *we have become trapped **in our own faith pursuits!***

We have become trapped *into focusing upon ourselves and our own faith.*

We have become trapped **in the strength of our own faith we can muster up.**

And so, *in ministry also,* we have become trapped **in our own faith projects!**

Faith is not for something you are still reaching for and trying to obtain in the far distant future or even the near future!

Not even faith itself is something that you are still reaching for and trying to obtain more of.

It is not something, that if you try hard enough, and pray hard enough, and memorize enough scriptures that you will hopefully be able, by your efforts, to get more of in the future sometime!

No, listen, ***Faith is merely <u>seeing</u> and fully embracing what you already have!***

Faith is based upon *what you already have; not upon what you don't have!*

Faith is therefore not focused upon what you can still get!

You see, *while I have to exercise my faith* ***to get somewhere,*** I'm going to get nowhere!

I'll actually do better with some worldly life improvement course on positive thinking, or on managing finances, or how to make money in real estate, or the stock market, if I am trying to get somewhere with my life! And the list goes on and on when it comes to that; but it has nothing to do with faith! **That's not what faith is all about!**

But instead you see, *when I discover faith in terms of __what I already have__ then my future becomes unhindered and unlimited!*

...My day becomes unhindered and unlimited!

...My experience and expectation of what God can do and what God can use me for in my day is realized and released; *it is __set free__ and __increased__!*

That faith, so richly inspired within me by what I can __see__ with my spiritual eyes, *by what I __already have__ in Him,* **becomes the __energy__ of God that __stirs__ my spirit and awakens resources within me,** *and it causes me to leap upon the mountains with hind's feet!*

That kind of faith, **which comes by __revelation into the truth of what I already have__ in Him,** *__mobilizes me__, with my trust secure in His love,* and I am motivated to go for it *and go do exploits for Him and with Him!* I do great exploits *knowing that He is with me,* **and provision or whatever else I need** *follows me and finds me!*

Paul was occupied with *giving;* **not** *getting* **– He was occupied with preaching! He was occupied with proclaiming the Gospel!** *And he refused to get distracted from that!* **He**
40

refused to get caught up in some job description! He had no other occupation!

Sure, he was involved from time to time with a private business enterprise together with Pricilla and Aquila, but mostly, it was their business, *not his.* Pricilla and Aquila often went ahead of Paul to a new city they wanted to go and do outreach in. And they would set up their little tent-making business, make friends and contacts in the community, share the gospel and wait for their companions and fellow servants in the gospel, Paul, and his team, to arrive. At times, Paul came alone and at times he came with his team. At times he joined them in making tents together, *but not always, not every time.*

You see, Paul never became Paul the tent maker! That never became his focus or identity! Making money in business or through ministry never became his focus! He remained Paul the apostle. **His heart was *occupied* with the gospel, not with some occupation or means of making money.**

At times he did what was necessary to sustain his natural life, to help provide for him and his team, *so as not to become a burden to others.*

He walked in a sensitive love relationship to his companions and to those he ministered to, but *they never became his source!*

Sure, they often supplied in his needs out of love for him and a desire to see this gospel go forth to reach the ends of the earth. *But as far as he was concerned, he loved them enough to not become a burden to them and put that expectation on them.*

Whatever they gave him, he wanted it to come from their heart, from the genuineness of love and no other motivation!

He steered clear of unhealthy expectations, especially when it came to money, because it could easily ruin relationships and become a stumbling block, especially to new believers who were young in the things of God and not given over to love yet.

Paul often worked with his own hands to provide for himself and for his team, in order *to not become a burden to anyone.*

He often labored to the point of exhaustion and even beyond the point of exhaustion, **all because of his passion for the truth and the purity of the gospel to be preserved in those who heard his message and looked to him for an example.** *He did it because of love!*

He says,

"I labored more than them all, yet not I, it was the grace of God that was with me!"

He did what he did for the sake of the gospel, **because of love.**

He labored much, when necessary, for the sake of the gospel, *but a job description never defined him or ruled him, nor restricted his life either!*

He was so given over to the passion alive inside of Him that he would have rather suffered if he had to, *even neglecting his own needs, if the situation called for it ...But when he was pressed to go and to move on, he went, **sometimes at great personal cost,** and he kept going **regardless of personal sacrifice.***

He didn't allow personal sacrifice to get in the way of going!

He was occupied with the gospel, *with sharing that gospel and making it plain and understandable to those who hadn't heard it in clarity yet, so that they too, could have an opportunity to respond to the truth and to God, intelligently and from the heart!*

His heart was so occupied with the gospel and he was so motivated and compelled by that love, propelled and driven even, *that he often suffered much in the going,* and all that just to be able to share and make known the gospel to people who hadn't heard it. ***He was occupied with sharing and proclaiming the gospel! He refused to be held back by fear and by money or the lack of it! He refused to be ruled by any fear or by money or by any job!***

That, then, is also the reason he wasn't married, because he knew that to some degree a married man *has to care for the things of his wife* and vice versa.

But He knew that he was fully caught up in the passion of the gospel and didn't want that interrupted, and so he made a decision to remain single *so that he could totally be a love-slave,* not in covenant-commitment and marriage to any other person, but *to Jesus and His cause exclusively!*

Paul was not against marriage. In fact, many of the apostles were married, *and they had to figure out how to yield to the passion of their hearts and continue in ministry, and in the preaching of the gospel, while at the same time taking proper care of their wives and their children!*

Listen; just like in a number of countries today, back then, your life and the lives of your wife and children were in danger if you were in ministry promoting the gospel, *and who wants to put their family through that?*

So often, back then, they as a family came into agreement and sacrificed together big time, just to be able to continue in ministry, as I am sure many families in ministry today still does!

My wife and I have made our own similar love agreement, and I thank God for her and her maturity in love, sacrificing like she does for me and for the sake of the ministry. It takes an exceptional person to go on that kind of love adventure with you. And I love, adore, and appreciate her for it. *Sometimes I love her so much, I feel like my heart is going to explode!*

Ha… ha… ha…

She truly is my life-companion! We serve and sacrifice for each other all the time in many ways *and we both have decided to put Jesus and the gospel first!*

But I still walk sensitive to her needs and I protect her from harm and too much hardship, and I lighten her burden whenever the things in life and ministry get too intense, and I spoil her when I can, and sometimes even when we can't really afford it. *And she does the same for me!*

But let's get back to Paul's ministry and the point I was making: **Faith is based upon <u>what you already have</u>! *Faith is <u>seeing</u> what you already have!* Faith is not focused** upon **what you can still get! *Love is seeing and appreciating and enjoying <u>what you already have</u>! Love is focused on that abundance!* Love is not focused on sacrifice! If it is seen as a sacrifice; *it's not <u>love</u>!* The love of Christ constrained Paul. The Greek word is the word, SUNECHO meaning, it resonated so deeply and so strongly with Paul that it kept echoing louder and louder within his, sweeping him** along in its wake, in its vortex, carrying him along on a journey, on the greatest of adventures, all *because he had come to the right conclusion in the gospel!*

The truth of God's love *inspired* him; it *compelled* him!

Love Himself compelled Paul!

And no he wasn't driven; *he went out with joy and was led forth in peace!*

Love; that romance of the ages, was his motivation!

Love was his sole motivation! Therefore, Paul was occupied with preaching! He was occupied with proclaiming the Good News!

And he refused to get distracted from that!

He refused to get caught up in some job description! He had no other occupation!

He also refused to get caught up in any other ministry distractions! He refused to get caught up in faith projects! Jesus didn't get caught up in any so called *"faith projects"* either. *Neither of them ever got caught up in building projects, and trying to build big ministries, and the whole nine yards!* Their focus wasn't buildings and seeing how many people they can fit under one roof on a Sunday morning. No! *Their focus remained fixed on the gospel; on imparting the truth of the gospel to people.*

When Jesus said: *"I will build My Church;"* He was not referring to building buildings. **He was talking about building an understanding of the truth of the gospel, an understanding of Sonship, and understanding of their true identity as children of God into people's hearts and minds;** *building people up in the very faith of God.*

Hey, we are all being built together into a holy habitation of God in the Spirit.

Paul also asks, *"Do you not know that you are the temple of the Holy Spirit."*

Listen; **YOU are God's favorite dwelling space;** *His abiding place,* not some temple in Jerusalem or some building we refer to as a *"church."*

God is building a household of faith. He is building His family. *He is calling all His lost kids into reconciliation and intimate relationship with Him.* **He is building up His sons and daughters with the truth of the gospel;** *He is restoring and rebuilding His image and likeness in them!* **He is restoring them to their original true identity,** *to the fullness of the measure of the stature of Christ, already within their spirits.* **That is what God is doing right now.** <u>**That's His sole focus**</u>**. That's what He is building! That's what** *"Church"* **is all about!**

So, rather than doing our own thing and focusing on building our own little ministries and our own little kingdoms, and what we think *"church"* is supposed to be, **why don't we join God in what He is doing and what He is building instead?!**

You see, that faith so richly inspired in me, by what I <u>see</u> with my spiritual eyes; *by what I already <u>have</u> in Him,* **that FAITH of God,** *takes me beyond religious ministry ambitions,* **and beyond my own personal needs even!** It takes me beyond *"holding my thumbs"* for a better car! I'm no longer sitting around, *waiting supposedly on God,* and trying to believe for that new building, or for that provision to finally arrive, *before I can move forward in ministry and do exploits!*

No!

The faith of God comes into my spirit with a new confession, saying, *'**God I desire the nations! They are my inheritance, not houses and buildings and lands and cars!**'*

'I thank you that we will have property and buildings and houses, but they are just temporary needs, they are just convenient meeting places, they only serve to advance the kingdom, Father!'

'A car is just a temporary need, Father. I mean, it is just meant to fill a need. The function of any car is just to get me from point A to point B. Father, I don't need a Mercedes
48

or a BMW to do that! A reliable car is a convenient necessity, that's all it is! Father, I won't attach any more value to it than that. I won't attach anything more to it! I refuse to see it as a status symbol! And so, a used one will do just as well; I don't need a new one, and I most certainly don't need all that debt that comes with it! I refuse to make a new car the pursuit of my life, Father! Thank you Father that my identity and fulfillment is not in that! Life is more than food and clothing! Father, You said: 'A man's life is not found in the things he possesses!' And so I thank You that my life is not found in name brand items or the latest fashion! Life is not found in the abundance of those things! Thank you Father, life is not found there, Father, my fulfillment is not found there! That is not my inheritance Father; those things are not my inheritance! **The nations are my inheritance and they are at my doorstep!**'

'**God I see a faith in my spirit, a new persuasion, and a new inspiration; a new love Father; a new passion; I see a new persuasion and a passion large enough to hold the nations in my heart, large enough to accommodate the nations, Father; large enough to take those nations!**'

Listen, God desires to awaken **His faith** in you! And let me tell you, *once you discover and taste the faith of God,* **you'll settle for nothing less!** There is no other alternative faith available on the *"Christian Market"* **that can** *possibly satisfy the way God's faith satisfies.* There's nothing that can compare or compete with the way God's faith and love satisfies!

Nothing can compare or compete with the satisfaction of seeing yourself from His point of view; with the joy of seeing the nations from His point of view!

Nothing can compete with God's faith when you begin to see your neighbor from His point of view, when you begin to see your wife, or your husband, or your mother-in-law ha... ha... ha... from His point of view!

There is a pleasure and an enjoyment in that which cannot be topped by anything in this natural world or by anything this life in the flesh has to offer!

You see, His faith and love **becomes that abundant life** *and the energy that mightily inspires you and empowers you from within!*

Now that is LIFE in Christ Jesus!

Chapter 4

Tapping in to God's Ability!

There is another Scripture I want to draw your attention to there in the last chapter of Romans. I'm reading to you from Romans 16:25,

"Now to Him who is able..."

Do you doubt God's ability? I mean, you don't need to have much theology behind you *to discover that God is omnipotent.*

As a little boy I used to wonder what that word *"omnipotent"* meant. And then I heard and discovered once that it meant that **there is nothing He cannot do!**

But the more edu-me-cated I became, His omnipotence became such a far out theological concept *that it was difficult to relate His omnipotence to my personal, practical now needs!* That's when you might as well know that *you have gathered too much head knowledge and not enough revelation, not enough heart knowledge,* and it is robbing you from the simplicity that is in Christ! **There is a simplicity in knowing and believing the love God has for you personally** *that no Christian can afford to ever lose!*

How do we discover *His omnipotence* in our personal experience? How do we *tap in* to **God's ability to work and do within us and through us?**

Paul says,

*"Now to Him who is able **to strengthen you according to my gospel**..."*

I like the Greek word used there for *"strengthen".* It's STERIKSON, and it means **to establish**, **to settle** you, **to root** you!

*"...**according to my gospel**"*

I praise God for Paul's gospel!

You see, there were various versions of the gospel on the market to choose from, even in Paul's days! And so Paul didn't want to limit the people's understanding to just kind of think of the *"gospel"* in general terms, in terms of everything that religion has to say about what they think the *"gospel"* is. Listen, the *"good news"* doesn't become that good anymore when you listen to every version of the gospel on the market! In fact, it turns into bad news!

Paul is saying there in Romans 16:25 that God's ability to work and to **do** in your life, His ability *to establish and strengthen you* in your own experience of Him, *is directly related to His gospel!* It is related to **this specific gospel,** the gospel which is **according to the revelation, or according to the incarnation**

of God in the flesh, in Jesus Christ, and His work of redemption accomplished in Jesus ...It is according to **that <u>revelation</u>; *to that <u>unveiling</u> of truth, to that unveiling of God's eternal truth!*** ...It is according to **the <u>proclamation</u> of that <u>exact</u> eternal truth, precisely *as <u>revealed in Jesus</u>!***

Paul says,

*"God's ability to work and do within you, to establish and strengthen you <u>is related to my gospel</u>, to this gospel, this exact revealed eternal truth and **its influence, its affect** upon you, **within you,** and it's effect within your life!"*

Romans 16:25,

"Now to Him who is able to strengthen you <u>according to my gospel</u> WHICH IS the preaching** (the proclamation) **of Jesus Christ..."

What is the proclamation of Jesus Christ?

Paul says,

*"...**it's according to <u>the revelation</u> (the unveiling)** ...of the mystery"*

You see, sometimes we think the *"gospel"* **is just proclaiming Jesus!** And then we go back into the gospels and we just relate historically and we begin to reminisce and talk sentimentally about His birth, His youth, His baptism, His temptation in the wilderness, and

His miracles, and His wonderful life, and His sad sad death, and His resurrection, and His ascension back into Heaven to go and be with His Father. And we think we've preached the Gospel. **Yet the mystery has not been revealed; the faith of God has not been preached and imparted.** *No genuine faith has been inspired!* Only about as much faith as it takes to believe in Napoleon has been inspired, because we just listen to an academic, historical account!

Listen, the Gospel that releases God's ability to energize your faith *and awaken that force within you that will take you beyond natural ability and talent is, "...according to the revelation of the mystery that has been hidden in God and kept secret in ages past."*

Did you notice the **past tense** there in that statement? Let's read it again, and I want it to really sink in deep in our understanding.

Romans 16:25,

"Now to Him who is able to strengthen you <u>according to my gospel</u>, which is, the proclamation of Jesus Christ, according to <u>the revelation</u> (or the <u>unveiling</u>) of the mystery <u>that has been</u> hidden in God and kept secret in ages past."

There is no reason why any believer today, any person really, *should still be living in a mystery concerning God and the way He relates to them!*

God's desire is to so unveil what He has said to us in Jesus Christ *that religion will no longer be able to rob us!* It will no longer be able to keep you blind and rob you **with its mere sentimental appreciation** of what happened over 2,014 years ago. **Your freedom is in *the revelation* (the unveiling) *of the mystery!***

Hallelujah!

Sometimes you listen to teaching *and the mystery becomes even more mysterious.*

Ha… ha… ha…

Someone once said about theologians (*and while there are some wonderful theologians out there that actually help us understand better,* **there are also some weird and wonderful ones out there!**) Ha… ha… ha…

So, someone once said about them, *'**You know, they seem to answer questions that are never asked in the first place!**'*

Hey, if you want to complicate the gospel for yourself friends, *then you just keep listening to them, okay?* You just listen long enough to that head knowledge stuff, that sense knowledge information about the Bible, and I can personally guarantee you that you'll get so confused that you're going to have to read some more commentaries and ideas, *and then most likely get even more confused, and end up shipwreck in your faith!*

But hey, no! Listen; it is <u>this</u> gospel, according to the revelation of the mystery, according to what God accomplished in Christ, which *releases God's ability to establish you,* **so that you are no longer tossed to and fro with every wind of doctrine that is the latest on the spiritual market.**

It is <u>*this gospel,*</u> *God's gospel, God's version of the gospel, according to His revelation or unveiling of the mystery,* which Paul identifies himself and his ministry with!

It's a gospel *that comes from God Himself, from God alone, from the revelation (from His unveiling) of the mystery!*

Do you understand what *"a revelation of a mystery"* means?

It means that **if there was a riddle <u>*it has now been solved*</u>***!*

It means that **if something was hidden <u>*it is now revealed*</u>***!*

In the next chapter I will briefly explain and unveil the mystery that has been hidden, *and lost in time;* that mystery that has been in God from before time began, *and has now been revealed in the fullness of time,* **in Christ Jesus; in God's work of redemption.**

But you would do well to also read my books on *God's Love For You!* and *God's Inheritance in You!* and perhaps *God's Eternal Purpose! And definitely also the series on: The Gospel in 3-D!* **to get a better understanding of the gospel;** *of what the gospel actually is.*

Chapter 5

No More Riddles and Mysteries, Just Clarity!

Listen, Paul is not expecting us to build our faith upon some weird and wonderful, confusing *mystery!* Paul is not expecting that of us! Neither is the Holy Spirit expecting any believer, or any other person for that matter, *to just step out into some kind of blind-fold experience with God!* The Christian life is not some weird and wonderful *confusing mystery!* True Christianity is not some weird religious *mystery!*

Especially among Pentecostal and Charismatic circles, *the Christian Church and the Christian Faith has become an emotional roller-coaster ride; a circus, and many who are of the Pentecostal and Charismatic persuasion are becoming more and more weird and spooky by the day,* **and it pains me to say so,** because I consider myself a part of that group, **but lately we have not really been on the same page.**

That's why I avoid labels as much as possible, and I associate with all Christians everywhere, *because there really is only one body, one Lord, one faith, and one immersion into that faith.*

I really dislike being painted into a corner and put in a box, that's why I hate and avoid being labeled **as anything** *other than* **a child of God.** My wife and I are just Christians *who understand and believe the message of the Bible, the prophetic message of the Old Covenant prophets pointing to Christ, and the prophetic writings of the New Testament apostles,* **unveiling the mystery concerning that Christ and His work of redemption, and concerning us, our true identity**.

Carmen and I, and our friends, our local body of believers here, and our other friends also who understand the true message of Grace, do believe in the gifts and the workings of the Holy Spirit, *and that it is for today,* **because the Bible teaches that it is for us**. **But we have come to understand that it is merely an outflow of the message, not something to pursue instead of the message, or in addition to the message!** *It only serves as confirmation of the message!* Just as the Scriptures also say:

"God does confirm His word with signs and wonders following!"

So I guess we are Pentecostal, or Charismatic, or whatever you want to call us. *But we are not part of the weird and spooky ones, ha... ha... ha...* What I mean is: *We still love them, they are still a part of us, part of the body of Christ; they are still part of the family,* **but we are not going to join them in their folly.** We are not going to join the ones that have turned into circus clowns and are on an emotional merry-go-round or roller-coaster ride *and growing more and more weird and spooky by the day!* **They somehow think that *the more mysterious they can picture their experience* the more spiritual they are! And also, *the more confused you get your audience,* the greater the impact of your message!**

But I'm not interested in their spookiness! I don't care if they've been to the third heaven and back, *or even the seventh heaven for that matter; pleading their own case in the courts of heaven!* I don't care if they have supposedly visited the throne room, *and even seen God on His throne!* Their experience adds nothing to clarify the Gospel, *it only veils it even more and distracts from it!*

Listen, I too have had my own experiences with God, numerous ones, but I don't care to let you in on it; those experiences were sacred to me, and so, I won't tell you all about it, because not only is it between me and the Lord but, *it won't enhance your faith either, or clarify the gospel one bit!*

Boasting about those experiences and comparing my experiences to yours, trying to figure out those experiences and trying to figure out whose experience was the greatest so that we can figure out who's more spiritual and who outranks whom, *gets none of us anywhere!*

I don't care how good your experience was, **it's just one big huge distraction from the gospel,** *and only leads to more and more confusion and spookiness to where no one can even relate to you anymore!*

If we can't relate to normal human beings anymore, because we are too spooky spiritual, and we lose them as an audience to the gospel; unable to understand and embrace the clarity and simplicity of the gospel, because they do not understand what the heck we're talking about, <u>we disqualify our ministry</u>!

You see, I want us rather ***to discover,*** *not some spooky spirit realm,* ***but the very basis of our appropriating. I want us to discover the basis, the truth, the very foundation, of our appropriating. I want us to discover what God revealed and did in Christ in simplicity!*** **Because until we discover THAT we will only get weirder and more spooky.**

...And ***our own efforts,*** to somehow try and **see** into that unseen realm of reality, *will continue to hamper our experience, and keep it limited to the weird and spooky and mysterious,* **instead of bringing us into *more clarity and understanding ...and an experience of real substance, as a*** *consequence ...which* will actually result in fruitful labor in the gospel!

Listen, I don't care how real your experience was! **Just because it was real, *does not mean it has actual substance!***

Paul made this powerful statement, he said,

"...even if an angel from heaven were to come to you..."

(Boy what a powerful, real experience!)

But he says, *"...even if an angel from heaven were to come to you with another interpretation of what the gospel is, with another gospel, other than the gospel we preach and proclaim, reject him!"*

He says: **Reject that experience!**

He says: ***That experience means nothing!***

So, I don't care how powerful that experience was to you, *it cannot add anything to your life!* It's of no value!

...Because it wasn't birthed out of insight and understanding in the first place, and in the second place, instead of grafting you in, *it ends up cutting you off even further!*

The Greek uses the word ANATHEMA, **to be cut off from the grace of God; *cut off from the favor of God!***

In other words, that experience actually causes you *to miss out on the grace of God,* to miss out on that <u>focus</u> you will need to maintain, *in that favor of God* <u>*already shown you and given to you*</u> *in Christ Jesus!*

It cuts you off in your experience of His favor and His fullness! Because <u>another focus</u> is emphasized; *another gospel is being preached.* And that lying focus; *that other gospel that is introduced* produces distance and separation again, *because it reintroduces confusion again instead of clarity!* It makes you again have to pursue after something <u>more</u>, *something <u>else</u>,* in <u>addition to</u> the truth, and the clarity, and the satisfaction and fulfillment of the gospel! It becomes a major distraction *and there is no way God can find any pleasure from it!*

God only finds pleasure in what the truth embraced in our hearts produces in us and in our lives as an experience!

God is only pleased when we experience the truth and what it produces!

The truth revealed in the gospel is the only thing of real value! It's the only experience, the only thing *that adds real substance, actual, tangible substance* to our lives!

Otherwise we keep living *in perpetual emptiness* until our next spooky spiritual experience; until our next weird and wonderful supposedly spiritual experience!

The truth revealed in the gospel is the only thing, the only experience that brings *tangible substance and actual lasting fulfillment, to our hearts and our lives!*

Let's get back to our Scripture. Paul says very confidently that, *"…**my gospel is the preaching of Jesus Christ.**"*

And now we can say,

*'So what, Paul. There are many people preaching Jesus Christ! What makes your gospel, your particular preaching of Jesus Christ **so much better** than theirs? What makes it **so much more special?**'*

What is it in his proclaiming of Jesus? I mean, if he is only proclaiming Him from a human point of view as a unique individual, as the greatest man that ever lived, or even as the unique Son of God, **as long as Jesus is still being preached as a unique individual, *separate from us,*** *or detached from that work of redemption,* **detached from our salvation***, then his gospel would not be any different than what all the other guys out there are preaching!*

You see, there has been a lot of preaching about Jesus Christ by many many preachers, *but they've kept Him in a shop window, in a display-only-window!*

*'Oh, but sorry for interrupting you brother Rudi, the Scriptures say, "We behold him as in a glass **dimly!**"'*

No friend, it does not! The Greek actually says that **as we behold Him _as in a mirror_ we are enlightened, and we are complete!** (2 Corinthians 3:18; Colossians 2:9 &10)

...Our thinking is transformed as we discover what is revealed;* as the truth revealed there concerning us *dawns on us!

If you don't understand the mystery revealed there in Jesus, you will keep preaching Jesus, *beholding Him,* **not as in a mirror** *but as in a glass box, a glass container, a display-only-window!*

And so, you sentimentally behold His death, you behold His miracles, and you sentimentally appreciate every bit of it, *everything that God did in Jesus,* **without understanding its vitally legal eternal content and implications!**

...You are beholding Him, alright, but **without comprehending how fully included the human race were in what God Himself achieved in the incarnation and work of redemption on our behalf and for our enlightenment!**

...It is no use beholding Him, ***without grasping what God actually revealed there concerning us, in His Son, Jesus!***

66

So Paul says here that,

*"...**my preaching of Jesus Christ, is according to the revelation (the unveiling) of the mystery.**"*

Hallelujah!

And what is that mystery?

Righteousness **as a gift!** That is the mystery revealed. Righteousness **by God's faith** and that faith alone.

That is the mystery revealed: **Our original righteousness is restored to us by the faith of God!**

That is what that mystery is all about: **God's true identity and our true identity, fully revealed and therefore also fully restored in Jesus Christ!**

God revealed Himself clearly there, in Christ and His incarnation and work of redemption!

He revealed Himself to be **Love!**

He revealed Himself to be **our Father;** *our one and only true Daddy!*

He revealed Himself to be *the One who loves us unequivocally and unconditionally!*

He revealed Himself to be *the One who has no judgment in His heart towards us!*

"God was in Christ when He reconciled the wayward world back to Himself, not imputing their trespasses to them!"

He is love and nothing else!

His heart, who He really is, was clearly revealed there!

And who we really are, *was clearly revealed there;* how He sees us, as Man united with God, as His offspring, His very own sons and daughters. That is what was clearly revealed there!

Our innocence restored to us; *that righteousness.* That is what was clearly revealed and restored to us there *in Jesus; in God's work of redemption!*

Your value and worth to God, as well as your real design and true identity, was clearly revealed in Jesus Christ, *and then redeemed and restored in full,* in the successful work of redemption!

The truth about God, His righteousness, and the truth about us, our original and authentic design, our true identity; our righteousness, was on display there in Him. *It culminated in that work of redemption!*

Hallelujah!

Do you know what has kept religion in darkness?

68

They have become stuck in a perpetual guessing game of *how to find God's approval,*

*...*because they remain focused **on their own efforts and their own works and their own conduct.**

They keep asking and keep wondering, *'How does Man, how do I, find God's approval?'*

You see, Job's friends challenged him again and again with that same question:

'Can a mortal man be innocent before his Maker? Can a man really be just before God; can a man truly be totally innocent?'

The devil has exploited that question *more than any other lying principle ever taught under religion!*

Religion has exploited that question about *Man's standing before God* more than anything else, *more than any other lie that has ever been taught as truth in religion!*

So Paul tells us that *the revelation of this mystery, **that revelation** of the mystery **is the revelation of how totally and legally Man was identified in Jesus Christ's death on our behalf!**

That revelation *of the mystery* **is the revelation on how completely we were all included in a death like His!**

So that when I **now** look at Christ I no longer see Him in a mysterious, weird, spooky, distant fashion!

But no, I am totally seeing Him <u>as in a mirror</u>!

I am seeing myself co-crucified in His cross!

That fallen identity co-died with Him!

And I, my original true self; my true identity was raised to newness of life in Him!

You see, that revelation *fuels your faith!*

It's what *"fires up"* your faith!

It is the source of true Christian faith and fire and pure passion!

Chapter 6

We Are Not Dealing With Some Post-Dated Promise!

Romans 16:25,

"...it was kept secret for long ages..."

Without going into too much detail, let me just quickly say that in Galatians Chapter Three Paul talks about *how after long ages* God began to instruct Man again about His original design, *about that quality of life He intended for Man from the beginning.* He began to help Man discover that there indeed was a quality of life beyond his own achievement. God, in the Law, began to help Man discover the extent and the nature of his dilemma in order to prepare them, *like a school teacher would prepare a child,* **for the fullness of time!**

And then Paul says in Chapter Four *that **the fullness of time has come!*** And he talks about **what God was able to reveal and to say to us in Christ!**

Okay, read with me now Romans 16:26,

*"...**my gospel; my preaching of Jesus Christ is related to the revelation of the mystery which was kept secret for ages.**"*

*"...it was kept secret in the long ages past ...**but it is <u>now</u> disclosed**..."*

Do you have a *"now"* there in your Bible?

Would that *"now"* be *of any practical value to you* right now?

Hallelujah! Ha... ha... ha...

You know, if we were dealing with some kind of post-dated promise, *and we suddenly discovered that the date in the right hand corner of the check **has come into fullness of time,*** would that affect your appreciation of the promise? **Sure it will!**

I mean, while the promise is there, *we can kind of in a way appreciate it sentimentally,* **because it's legal and it's real and it's vital. It is wonderful,** *but it's for tomorrow!*

But now, *if it's disclosed* that in the fullness of God's calendar, **in the fullness of eternity and time measure, God sent forth the Son,** *to redeem* **those who were being taught by the law, to bring them** *to fullness,* **and announce to them** *their coming of age, and confirm to them their sonship, and the love of their Father, and His approval of them, and their equal value, their equality to Jesus in relationship with the Father,* then a new *"now"* dawns upon your understanding!

Hallelujah!

Listen, a new *"now"* comes to you in the gospel! **A *"now"* that is bigger than your need!**

You see, Jesus came to introduce us to none other than **I AM!** *None other than EMANUAL;* **the God that is with us and in us always!**

Paul says in Romans 6:26,

"...my gospel; my preaching of Jesus Christ is related to the revelation of the mystery which was kept secret for ages;"

"...but is now disclosed;"

"...through the prophetic writings."

"...through both the prophetic writings of the Old Covenants and the New Testament."

Can you now see the value of the prophetic writings, *in terms of the value of that post-dated check?* The writings of old, that manuscript, that document *carried* **the thought of God** *for ages;* hidden there in a mystery. **It carried the promise of the Creator concerning His creation, concerning salvation,** *concerning us, His offspring.* **It carried that promise in a mystery box.**

Paul says, *"...but it is now disclosed..."*

"...and through the prophetic writings **(The New Testament prophetic writings)** *it is now made known to all nations."*

73

Hallelujah! Thank you Father; *thank you Holy Spirit!*

John sees Him in the book of Revelation and he says that He is surrounded. His throne is surrounded with those who are represented there; **multitudes upon multitudes of every nation, and every tribe, and every tongue known to Man!**

Multitudes upon multitudes of His creatures; of His children, of His offspring, giving Him a standing ovation!

Standing in adoration before Him *as a result of His adoration of them!*

They are His trophy! They are the fruit of the travail of His soul! They are the fruit of that work of redemption! They are the fruit of that truth revealed! They are the fruit of the impact of the gospel! They are the fruit of the impact of the revelation! They are the fruit of the embrace of that revelation, and of embracing that revelation within themselves!

They are the apple of His eye!

They are His loved ones!

Hallelujah!

Chapter 7

The Nations Are Our Inheritance!

You know, religion has duped us into thinking, *'Oh well, you know, the road is narrow and maybe it's just going to be a few here and there that's going to make it in there!'*

I thank God for the liberating truth of the gospel! I thank God for its narrow-minded focus upon the truth, upon the revelation of the mystery! In that revelation it is revealed that everyone is included! Those who have a heart to believe and a mind to understand, a spirit and a heart to grasp and comprehend and embrace these things, **they are the ones who enter in, to enjoy!**

*And they not only enter into the fullness of these things themselves, **but they understand that it is for everyone!***

Hey listen, **God had more in mind than the individual;** *than even just a few individuals!*

He has more in mind than just the individual! When He saw Abraham, He saw more than an individual, and so when He took Abraham out one night, He said, *'Abraham, I'm* *going to give you a glimpse of My plan for your life. I want to give you a little parable, so that you will never ever doubt again the size of My vision for you!' He said, 'Abraham, start counting stars!'*

Hey listen, you too, start counting the stars, *if you want to get a vision from God for your life!*

Do you know that there are **more** people alive today *than the amount of people that have ever died in the history of Man?*

In 1804, for the first time in the history of Man, Mankind's population reached 1 billion.

So, **from the beginning of time, it took all the way until 1804 for the world's population to even get to 1 Billion**... ha... ha... ha... now, isn't that something?

But now, look at this: In 1927, *a mere 123 years later,* from the beginning of time till 1804, and now suddenly, from 1804 till 1927 (I mean, how can you even measure and compare the time it took from the beginning of time till 1804, with a mere 123 years?) **In a mere 123 years** from 1804, in 1927, *the 2nd Billion appeared!*

And then **only 32 years later,** in 1959, the 3rd Billion!

Then **15 years later,** in 1974, there suddenly was 4 Billion people living on the planet! And we are now over 7 Billion, and estimated to reach 8 Billion in just 10 short years! Isn't that amazing?!

So let me say it again, so it can sinks in: **There are more people alive today on this planet *than have ever lived!***

Therefore the Church of the Lord Jesus Christ needs to be enlarged *in our understanding of the commission of that apostleship of His grace!*

Listen, God does not have a small work in mind! He doesn't have in mind: **you in your small corner, *and I in mine.***

Ha… ha… ha…

The Scriptures say,

*"**Get thee up into a high mountain, and lift up your voice with strength!***"

You've got something to say to the nations!

Their guilt is pardoned!

Listen; if one died for all, ***then all have died!***

One died for all, ***therefore, all have died!***

*"**THEREFORE** if any Man be in Christ, **he is a new creation!** The old things have all passed away **in His death! Behold all things are new! Now all these things are of God!** (**Of God are you in Christ!** – 1 Cor. 1:30)"*

"He has entrusted us with this revelation as a ministry! He has given us this ministry of reconciliation! That's the only legitimate ministry He has given us! Listen, God was in Christ! He reconciled the world to Himself!" - 2 Corinthians 5:17 & 18

That is exactly what birthed our ministry and became the substance of our message!

Verse 19 says,

"...in Christ God was reconciling the world to Himself, not counting their trespasses against them;"

"...and so He entrusted to us that message of reconciliation!"

God desires to increase the volume of His appeal to the nations *through your life!*

You are *the* essential part in God's strategy to reach this world with His appeal!

If faith is for anything it is for that!

...So that you can become the volume of the voice of God's appeal to the nations!

His faith sees nothing short of that for you!

Allow that faith to motivate you to proclaim and make plain His message, His good news to the people around you!

Allow His faith to become **that fuel within you** *that propels you into the ministry of reconciliation!*

Allow it to become the zeal; the necessary drive within you*, to commission you to go to the nations.*

Allow God's faith to become the energy within you *that enables you to run with the gospel!*

Allow it to become the inspiration within you *that He so mightily inspires within your heart to make you fall in love with people* ...*in love with people in general, in love with all kinds of people;* ***in love with the nations!***

Allow that faith of God, that love of God to come alive in your heart and to make you want to run to the nations with the gospel!

If you are going to believe God for anything, *believe Him for that!* ***Believe Him for the nations! Believe Him for your full inheritance, to come into that inheritance, and lay a hold of it fully!***

Listen; the nations are your inheritance; *the ends of the earth your possession!* Don't bother to believe God for a bigger home and a better car! Rather *get mobile in your heart and in your feet,* **and you'll have every vehicle, and every piece of property, and every home, and every building that this world has to offer at your disposal!** Get mobile in your heart, *commissioned through the grace that you have received!*

"...His grace towards me was not in vain!"

And so Paul appeals there in 2 Corinthians 6:1,

He says, *"Listen, I appeal to you that you receive His grace, not in vain!"*

In Galatians 5 he says,

"...why would you still continue to prefer your own efforts, your own works, to His grace?"

He says, *"...it's like putting yourself outside of the field of grace."*

"...you put yourself outside the reach of that grace!"

"...outside of its influence;"

"...outside of its affect!"

"...as if God's approval in Christ, as if God's grace is not sufficient enough!"

Romans 6:26, *"...my gospel; my preaching of Jesus Christ is the revelation of the mystery which was kept secret in long ages past, but is now disclosed and is now being made know to all nations."*

God sees nations in your faith, amen!

Chapter 8

Give Yourself Over to the Influence of Grace!

Do you see what a priority it is for us now...? I mean it's a **_big priority!_** I am telling you, **_it's a priority_ to discover in God's faith _that fuel_ which will inspire our faith _with such intensity_ that we will pour out our lives like a drink offering!**

We must discover in God's faith _the fuel_ _that will inspire our faith _with such passion_ that we who are equal with Him, in terms of the equality He accomplished for us in Christ, _that we now no more count our equality as a thing to be grasped at; to still try and obtain,_ or to hold onto just for ourselves, _but that we would have the same mind which was in Christ; that exact same heart, that mind-set!_ He made Himself of no repute; _He gave Himself!_ He fully gave Himself!

I don't believe that once this truth hits your heart; _once the love of God has been awakened in your heart through the truth of the gospel that **you'd ever need to have someone appeal to you for a contribution again!**_

I don't believe any of us *that have this light as a witness burning within us* **will ever again even consider giving reluctantly!**

'Well, I wonder how I can afford to give really. You know, I've kind of already worked out my budget and, oh, this is now so inconvenient, it is going to make it so complicated and I don't know how I'm going to be able to do this!'

Listen friend, *don't worry! Don't do it then!*

But when you begin to understand the gift of His grace, **allow that grace to silence fear and to begin to fuel you with love, with a new kind of faith! Allow it to fuel you** with a **new kind of vision!** *Not just for you and your four –* us four and no more! But for you, yes; **and also for the nations!**

Now in saying all this to you, I don't mean for you to leave your brain at the door **and to get so zealous about giving that you just start sponsoring any Tom, Dick, and Harry out there** *promoting any old kind of religious thing in the name of the gospel!* I'm not saying that! We who see the truth of the gospel clearly *must learn to promote this gospel exclusively! And that means sponsoring fully those who promote it and those who lay down their lives to go out and preach it with clarity; making known its full implications and its full intent to the nations!* It means we are not going to keep sponsoring religion **also,** *with its emphasis on* *works and* **on a person's own efforts** *to obtain what the truth of the gospel reveals they already have!* It means *we need to* **stop** *supporting* those who promote an inferior interpretation of the gospel!

We need to love them and try and bring them into a greater revelation of the truth of the gospel, yes; *but how can we in good conscience keep sponsoring the proclamation of an inferior gospel?*

I am saying that we who see the truth of the gospel clearly *cannot keep supporting all kinds of religious gospels!* **We cannot keep sponsoring all kinds of religious nonsense** *being sold to people in the name of Jesus as the gospel,* **when, in fact, we know that that stuff being preached** *is not the gospel and ends up working against the gospel,* **just like weeds in a garden, hampering any healthy growth, or worse yet, choking the life out of everything in the garden!**

It only perpetuates ignorance and the authority and influence of darkness! It perpetuates that ignorance! It perpetuates religion, that man-made thing! *It truly only serves* **to undermine the truth of the gospel!**

And I don't care what you have been taught about tithes either! *We must learn to support the true gospel and its true ministers exclusively!*

When you begin to understand the gift of His grace more fully, you will also understand what I am talking about! **I am not preaching rebellion! I am merely saying,** *place appreciation and value where it really belongs!*

God has called us to undo and reform religion. He's called us *to transform that man-made thing from the inside out;* not to perpetuate it! I believe I am writing, not from a rebellious heart, but from a heart filled with true appreciation and value and therefore passion *for the things **God places value upon!***

...I believe I am writing, not from my top five inches right now, *certainly not from any kind of religious thinking right now, ha... ha... ha... but I'm writing to you straight from the heart of God!*

*Listen, God wants us to promote and sponsor His true gospel exclusively; **and not any other kind of gospel, amen!***

The faith of God wants to fuel and inspire our faith to the point *where we not only give generously,* **but to where we go beyond giving of just our finances,** *and we actually begin to give ourselves,* **and pour ourselves out as a drink offering upon the altar of other's faith;** *upon the service of that faith coming alive* **in them also, inspiring God's faith in them!**

See, God is after your whole heart, *not just your money,* amen!

Ha… ha… ha… Hallelujah!

Thank you Jesus! Thank you Father for such a great commission! Thank you that it's *our portion!* Hallelujah!

Listen, Jesus gave Himself fully! He made Himself of no reputation! **He laid down His life!**

…And Paul himself got so raptured, *so caught up in the heart of God, so involved in the mission of God,* that he said, *"I wish that I myself was accursed and cut off for the sake of my brethren!"*

Hey, that's love!

He got so persuaded in the revelation, so caught up in it! *He got so captivated and engaged in the love of God, so involved in the mission of God.* And we see how the compassion of God begins to take him to <u>the same measure</u>, *to the stature of the fullness of Christ!*

Paul got so caught up in the revelation, so captivated and engaged in the love of God; in the truth of the gospel that *it took him to that same measure of love;* that same mature love measure, *in the laying down of his life also!*

85

The truth of the gospel took Paul to the exact stature of the fullness of Christ *in which He, in love, laid down His life for us!*

Paul began to walk in that, *to live his life energized and motivated and mobilized from within by the love of Christ* in order to make fully known to the understanding of the nations the principle of selfless unselfish devotion.

It's where I give myself beyond any measure of Man! Beyond calculation! Beyond budget! Beyond needs even! Beyond looking at it as a sacrifice! All because of the compelling of His grace, the beauty and appeal of His truth and of His love! All because of that compelling influence within me; His compelling influence, the compelling influence of His grace and of His apostleship.

The grace of God and that apostleship; the compelling influence we become entrusted with, desires to take more than just the town we live in, more than just a few more families for our Church fellowship, but to go beyond the borders. And it makes you say, *'God, there is a nation out there that belongs to You, and it belongs to me, it's got my name on it! And there are nations upon nations out there that belong to You!*

...They are all included in the same love sacrifice!

...And God, they are our inheritance!'

Listen, God sees the most ignorant heathen **in the same light as He sees you!**

He sees them **with that same love** and with **that same compassion!**

Chapter 9

Take the Limits Off of God and Yourself!

I've got 2 granddaughters now in the flesh. And you know, so often we become conditioned to think in terms of how many children are we really going to have? And for parents it becomes quite popular to have two, I know, *but not for grandparents!*

Ha... ha... ha...

I remember after our first grandbaby I thought, *'God, where are we going to get all our love from now, because we have already given all our love to our little Isabelle, and now there's another one on the way. Where are we going to get that much love from? I mean, we've given everything we've had!'* But when Gabrielle was born, we discovered the most delightful parent and grandparent principle. We discovered within ourselves a capacity, a parent and grandparent capacity *that went beyond measure!* The most difficult thing for Carmen and me now is to keep our mouths shut and not beg the kids too much to not stop at just two grandbabies!

Ha... ha... ha...

If they stop now, how many others could still be there? I mean, Charles Wesley was the 16th child!

Ha… ha… ha…

Relax, alright. We've been assured, despite our best efforts, *they do not intend to follow our suggestions any further!*

Ha… ha… ha…

Wow, what a Church growth plan!

Ha… ha… ha…

But listen, I do want to say this to you: You don't need to take any *caution* when it comes to reproducing yourself in faith! God doesn't want to see you limited to just 12 disciples, so don't get religious on that number okay! Jesus had infinitely more than 12 in mind; *otherwise you wouldn't have been here!*

He says,

"The works I do, you will do, <u>and greater</u>!"

Because He understands the principle of multiplication! God sees a potential in your faith-experience that will multiply beyond number!

"…Jerusalem shall be without walls!"

Just a couple of months ago I was struggling, and I was wrestling within myself, as we sometimes do when we are going through a hard time, or when we are challenged by doubts and fears, and accusations from the enemy. I was trying to deal with anxiety within myself, but I knew what the Lord says for us to do during those times when we face various trials and temptations and burdens that do not come from Him.

And so I began to pray and meditate upon my Daddy's goodness and upon some of the prophetic words God has spoken over our lives and over our church-body in the past. And it began to dawn on me that we have been getting an increase of similar words from people here more and more lately, in which God almost always says the same things concerning how He has called us to an international ministry, to impact the nations, and that it will come about through the disciples we take under our wing personally, and through the ones we raise up in our church-fellowship.

Now as I was meditating on these prophetic words and wondering how in the world God was going to make it all come to pass, I felt led to begin reading the Scriptures, and I just opened my Bible and began to read in Zechariah 2:1-12. And this is what it says,

"And I lifted my eyes and saw and behold a man with a measuring line in his hand. And

*then I said, 'Where are you going?' And he said to me, 'To measure Jerusalem, to see what its breadth is, and what its length is.' And behold the angel who talked with me came forward, and another angel came forward to meet him, and said to him, 'Run! Say to that young man, '**Jerusalem shall be inhabited as villages without walls!** Because of the multitude of men and cattle in it! For I will be to her a wall of fire round about her, says the Lord! And I will be **the very glory within her!'***"

You see, Jerusalem's beauty had to try and be defined by Man, because after all, *this is Jerusalem!*   Because every city carries its own pride!   Especially the city of Jerusalem! So Jerusalem had to have its measure by Man, lest you know, others should boast in her glory! And its politics would serve to so define its measure that only pure Jews would live in Jerusalem!

'Let's keep the Arabs out so that the Jews would be the glory of Jerusalem,' you see!

But then we've got some enemies, especially because of our policies and our politics, so we've got to do something else, something more you know. So, let's marry the two, you know, and while we are defining our boundary lines, *let's build large walls!* I mean, high enough walls *to keep the enemy out and us in!* **Until the walls become a prison of <u>frustration</u>, just like it did so many times in**

the history of Israel and the strategy of war in Jerusalem, when the very walls we trusted in; the very insurance policies we've taken out, <u>becomes a prison to us</u>, and it snares and captures us, *and we end up dying within those walls.*

But the minute I came across that Scripture and while I was reading it, *the Spirit of God began to quicken my spirit, and my heart began to burn within me so much, to such a degree that I could no longer sit there in my office.* I immediately began to become aware that *God Himself was dealing with **me** and speaking to **me,** and His voice echoing inside me became so intense that I could not stay there in His presence!* I had to get up and walk out of the room.

I just knew in my heart, deep within me, that God was saying something so significant and so profound *to me and to our ministry **and really to everyone called into the revelation of His grace and to the apostleship that comes with that revelation of grace!***

I went downstairs into our basement and ran right into a young man named Kenneth. He was standing there with a measuring tape, trying to measure the size of the basement and the distance between the ceiling and the floor. *I went ice cold!* I'm telling you, *I had goose-bumps running all up and down my spine!* You see, we were in the process of renovating the basement so that some young people who were joining our ministry could move into it. *For a moment I thought I was having a vision.*

Ha… ha… ha…

Because I just read about the young man with a measuring line, *and here I run right into Kenneth, standing there with his measuring tape.*

I grabbed him by the shoulders and said,

'Kenneth, stop your measuring! Stop it! Stop measuring that wall!'

I ran back up stairs and grabbed my Bible and I came back down stairs and I read to him that Scripture. ***And then I challenged him to stop measuring himself by his shortcomings and his failures and his unworthiness!*** **I told him how much God loves him and that He has already given him a different measure to measure his life by, and that he can stop measuring himself in the flesh now!**

He just looked at me with that bewildered look in his eyes! I don't think he quite knew what had gotten into pastor Rudi all of a sudden…

Ha… ha… ha…

But I didn't care! *And really I don't care anymore what others think of me!*

I bet he won't forget what I said though! *And he will probably have to keep wrestling with it in his heart for a while!*

Ha… ha… ha…

You see, we have embraced a gospel *with a commission* **and it's about time we get out of our four walls, the four walls of our church buildings, and get with God's agenda for His Church! It's about time we yield ourselves to the influence of His grace, *to the mobilizing influence of his truth and of His love!* Lift up your eyes, *the field is white unto harvest!***

That harvest has your name on it!

As I read that Scripture that morning, God said to me, *'**Rudi, don't you try and define your ministry and try and put a boundary around what I am about to do! Don't you dare start counting chairs and people and money or the lack of it! And don't you dare start comparing yourself and competing with other ministries! ...And, you know, trying to see who's actually got the most successful or biggest ministry in your area!'***

He said to me,

*"**Jerusalem shall be without walls! And I will be the glory within her!**"*

Listen, you don't need to try and protect your own identity! You don't need to try and protect your own doctrine; **your own definitions even!**

...**And you don't even need to try and defend your own reputation either if the Lord becomes your glory!**

He said to me,

'Son, I will be your reputation, I will be your glory, and I will be the wall of fire round about you and within you! Your enemies will not consume you! No weapon that they form against you will prosper! Every tongue that rises against you to condemn you will be refuted and rebuked! You just continue to be <u>secure</u> in My love and to walk <u>in love</u>, compelled <u>by My love</u> and <u>by My truth</u> and <u>by My grace</u>!'

So I want to say to you also who are reading this book: **Don't allow Man's opinion *to build a wall around your heart or around your life!*** Don't even allow your own desire to be someone, *to be something;* don't allow that empty human ambition **to restrict you and try to mold you,** *and become a stumbling block in your life, and so l<u>imit God's glory in your life</u>!*

Instead of you living with the glory of empty pride; *He wants to be the glory within!*

"And we have this glory in earthen vessels!"

Don't try and defend the earthen vessel! It's not about the earthen vessel! The earthen vessel has no value *outside of the glory that it carries!* It's the glory that gives it its value; its worth! **We carry the glory! And that glory,** according to 2 Corinthians 4:6 & 7, **is exactly related to the light; that revelation revealed, that light and truth about God and us, that shone in the face of Christ!**

That revelation that God shines into your heart **and releases into your understanding concerning the truth of the gospel,** *becomes your glory!* **It becomes your treasure, and the measure of your light! It becomes the measure of your life, and the measure of your ministry!**

Hallelujah!

I know that God has already spoken to you through this book, *and I want you to begin to measure yourself in terms of His broken flesh!* **You see, the only reason His flesh was broken** *was to open a new and a living way for you!*

The old way wasn't good enough!

The old religious system and the Law system weren't good enough! The Law couldn't do it and religion couldn't do it! The Law wasn't good enough! *It couldn't open that new and living way!*

The Law's emphasis; the emphasis of religion is **condemnation!**

I said that, because the Law and religion *restricted your contribution to your own ability to do,* **and therefore *to your own restrictive fears!* It restricted you to your fleshly needs, pride, and ambitions! It restricted you to** your own natural identity; *your warped search for identity!*

But grace extends to you now through His torn flesh! Grace comes to you! The gospel comes to you! His favor comes to you! That gospel of favor comes to you! The gospel of the heart of His love comes to you, *to silence your fears and to awaken your faith, and so, to awaken a different kind of obedience that goes beyond measure; it goes beyond reward or punishment!*

...And in that new kind of obedience awakened within you, your faith becomes the new measure, *the hand that receives His full measure!*

Chapter 10

Beyond Measure!

I wonder if I could just turn your attention quickly to 2 Corinthians 10. I wrote two other books also on *God's Measure versus Man's Measure,* and *No Longer Looking for Applause,* and I went into much more detail in those two books, so I encourage you to get them, but I just want to emphasize some of it here also.

When God gave us the vision and the strategy for discipling people we based it on Matthew 25 where Jesus used the parable of the talents of money and He talked about *multiplying what you have been entrusted with, **referring to the gospel.*** And we based it on that Scripture in Matthew 26 where we find the story of the woman who broke the alabaster box and how Judas was so offended *because he saw so much natural value in that alabaster box that he wanted to sell it for 300 pieces of silver.*

God spoke to us about the woman, the Church, the local congregation of believers, and *how every individual believer **needs to be given the opportunity to give beyond value!***

You see, that woman in Matthew 26, in one moment, gave a year's salary. She gave a whole year of her life in one offering, in one moment's sacrifice! No wonder that Judas was so upset. In that same chapter we also see him, supposedly one of Jesus' full time team, betraying Jesus and selling Him out for 30 pieces of silver; *a mere month's wages!*

You see, we have to pioneer a new definition of giving and serving in the local Church, *especially among us who understand the word of His grace and know that we have been entrusted with the stewardship of that grace.* **We must get rid of the hireling mentality and the greed and pride driven measure of religion,** *as well as the restrictive, limited fear measure of legalism and the Law.*

And in its place we need to develop a new mentality *that releases people,* **and then we need to give those people also** *the opportunity to become ministers of this gospel,* **and to give their lives to full time ministry;** *even if it is only for one year!*

We should give them an opportunity **to lay their lives down for Jesus and to lay down their lives in love for their fellow believers and for their fellow Man!** *So that in that they can experience the extension of God's commission through them!*

And then there is also the next Scripture that we base discipleship on. After God gave us the commission for discipleship, *then He also gave us this strategy there in 2 Corinthians 10!*

Paul says there in verse 12,

"Not that we venture to class or compare ourselves with some of those who commend themselves ...because when they measure themselves by one another and compare themselves with one another they are without understanding!"

What is it that they do not understand *that still causes them to measure themselves and others and even ministry by the wrong measure?*

You see, **they still see ministry as just another prestigious job opportunity, just another opportunity to promote themselves and to get ahead and to spiritually and naturally outdo the next guy! They still consider godliness as a means of gain!** What is it that they do not understand?

They do not understand *that **godliness with contentment is great gain!*** They do not understand that **contentment with godliness,** *or contentment with God-likeness; contentment with the image and likeness of God within them, contentment with being God's Child, contentment with enjoying intimate friendship and fellowship with Him **is gain! They do not understand that <u>that</u> is great gain!***

They do not understand *the correct measure of Man!* *They do not understand GOD'S measure* **of Man!** **They do not understand why He made Man!** *They do not understand that simply fellowship with Him, in <u>His</u> thoughts, in <u>His</u> truth, is great gain!* They do not understand **that intimate fellowship with Him, is great gain!** **That <u>He</u> is our exceedingly great reward!**

They really do not understand *the correct measure of Man!* *They do not understand GOD's measure of Man; the measure God has measured Man by, and the measure He has made us for!*

Therefore their whole prideful, greedy, competition mentality *is motivated by a measure that is totally inferior to God's measure of Man, totally inferior to God's measure of grace!*

They think there is *some merit* in their boasting, *some valid boasting in gathering so many people together in one building or in one place, or so many rich ones especially, or so many popular business people or any other kind of popular people in town even, so many famous ones especially.*

Hey, <u>**God**</u> **says,**

<u>"There's no merit in that;</u> there's no ground for boasting in that, because that's not the right measure! That's not the measure!"

Ephesians 4:7 says,

"Grace was given to each one of you according to the measure of Christ's gift."

And so 2 Corinthians 10:12 says,

"When they measure themselves by one another they are without understanding!"

And then verse 13 struck me just as hard.

He says,

"But as for us, we will not boast <u>beyond limit.</u>"

Actually that word *"limit"* used there is that same Greek word that is used for *"measure"*. Thus, it should read, *"But as for us, we will not boast beyond measure;"*

"…but we will keep to the measure God has apportioned us."

Or better yet,

"…we will keep to that same measure that God has measured us by!"

Paul uses that little Greek word for *"measure"* again and again. In other words, he says that, *'I will not be snared to get into another mold, or another measure, beyond, or outside of God's measure! …Beyond, or outside, His opinion of me!'*

And listen, God's measure of you is portrayed graphically in His Son Jesus Christ! **Nothing more, *nothing less!***

What we see in Him is our measure which God has measured us by!

He is: The fullness of Deity indwelling Him *in a human body!* The fullness of Deity, *therefore indwelling us!*

In Him there is all of God *in a human body!*

Can you begin to see the measure God has in mind for you; can you begin to see the measure He has <u>already</u> measured you by once and for all?

And so we see how Paul defends and justifies his ministry, *and he goes far beyond religious Church politics in the next verse.*

2 Corinthians 10:14,

"For we are not overextending ourselves in reaching you, as though you were not of value; as though you were not also included in Christ's work of redemption!"

I want you to notice that he was writing this letter to the Greeks. Yes, he was writing to everybody, *but to the Greeks at Corinth in particular!* You can go and study his strategy in your Bible, in the maps section in the back of most older Bibles, and you will find out exactly *where Greece is in relation to Damascus.*

And religious Church politics would have you start wondering, **'Is Paul not, perhaps, over-extending himself?'**

'I mean brother Rudi; you are pastoring a local Church, with hard working middle class families, struggling just to eke out a living for themselves and for their loved ones. **What makes you think they can accommodate such a large vision?**'

Hey listen, God has more for the local Church in mind than Jerusalem and its boundaries!

He says,

"...you will be My witnesses, both in Jerusalem, and in Judea, and in Samaria, and to the uttermost parts of the earth!"

Hey, how is that for boundaries?!

Ha... ha... ha...

And listen, if that's not our strategy *then we're deceiving ourselves!* The gospel can only be measured accurately by the ends of the earth! **The accurate conclusion of the gospel includes the ends of the earth!**

Through the years I have had so many people tell us, *'Brother, it seems to me; you guys just need to make up your minds in ministry, either you are a discipleship school or you are a local Church; either you're a mission or you are a Church, but you can't be both!'*

The problem is that I only find one strategy in the Bible and that is: *A Church <u>with a mission</u>; a commissioned Church!*

Jesus said, *"I will build my Church, and the gates of Hell will not prevail; it will not restrict it nor be able to contain it …and it won't be able to hold it back, or stop it from going forth either…"* Never mind the boundaries of South Carolina!

Ha… ha… ha…

Listen, He said the gates of HELL will not prevail against you! Never mind the war zones of this world! The gates of HELL will not prevail **against My Church!**

God wants to inspire you to go with what He says is available to you in the fuel of His faith in you! It is not related to who you are in the natural man; *whether you are of noble birth,* **or of no one's birth.** *Maybe you're an out-cast,* **but listen;** *He measures you in terms of His value that He places on you; in terms of that value that's <u>within</u> you <u>already</u>!*

Chapter 11

Not Overextending Ourselves!

Paul says in 2 Corinthians 10:13,

"For we are not overextending ourselves to reach even to you..."

Do you see that last line there in verse 13?

"...to reach even to you!"

Do you see that Paul sees clearly that this grace that compelled him, and hopefully now compels you, *includes not only your neighbor, not only your brother, in Pastor so-and-so's territory, but also the uttermost parts of the earth?*

Verse 14,

"For we are <u>not</u>..."

Listen to me now. If all the religious church etiquette and politic nonsense makes you nervous, Paul himself says,

"...we are <u>not</u> overextending ourselves!"

'Now, brother Rudi, aren't there already enough churches in the area and around the

world, even in most of those countries you are talking about going to?'

Hey, listen there are more than enough churches, *but how do you measure CHURCH?*

"...we are <u>not</u> overextending ourselves, as though we did not reach you. In fact we were the first to have come to you <u>all the way</u> with the gospel of Christ!"

Listen that means preaching the gospel in its full implications! Not just preaching a watered down gospel to be able to gather people on a Sunday and get their money to pay a salary and to pay off the buildings! ...**but, *preaching the gospel all the way!***

'Now, brother Rudi, why are you trying to proselyte others? Aren't you just trying to steal their sheep?'

Listen, there may be many religious faiths, ***but not all faiths are equal!***

<u>Faith</u> is only <u>faith</u> when it is the <u>faith of God</u>!

If it is not the <u>faith of God</u> *it is no <u>faith</u> at all!*

Faith is inaccurate if it is not the <u>faith of God</u>! And so, I don't care what religion you are part of, **faith, if it is not the <u>faith of God</u>, *is not a faith worth having!***

The <u>faith of God</u> needs to be clarified *because people's faith must be made accurate <u>if it is to be of any real good,</u> of any earthly good ...and for that matter, of any heavenly good; or any other good at all!*

If we are not dealing with **the faith of God** then we are merely dealing with Man-made religion!

Religion is no good!   Religion only appears to be good, but it is deception, and deception in the long run *steals, kills, and destroys!*

No religion can be compared to **the faith of God!** I say again: ***Religion cannot be compared to the faith of God!***

People don't need religion; **they need the faith of God!** And if people are busy with religion, **they need to be educated in the faith of God** so they can become free *and be free indeed!*

Listen; if someone's faith is inaccurate, they need help! God has sent us to help them **by imparting a more accurate faith to them** so that they can prosper in the purposes of God and come into their freedom more fully, *and come fully into that inheritance that is theirs in Christ Jesus!*

That includes both pastors and the flock God has made them overseers of!

I don't want to take those people out of their church! **I just want to transform those people's thinking *so that they can be*** *inspired* and go into their local church and help their pastor transform that local church and transform that community!

Now if the pastor feels threatened by that and prefers religion, *and throws them out or shuts them down and tries to put out their fire,* **then my advice to them would be to move on and shake the dust off of their feet and to not look back!**

And don't let your conscience bother you one bit about it either!

If they want to remain stuck in religion then don't you remain stuck with them!

I am not saying this to stir up rebellion, *but you can't function if you are unequally yoked!*

Go and find your own company, *people who* **embrace** *these things!*

And if there is no one in your area, *then start a Bible Study in your own home, and use one of my manuals, or start with a book or two,* **and let God use you to make friends and to minister and impart truth to your neighbors. Lead them to the truth of the gospel, and impact them with the love of God, and begin to pull together a body of believers in your area, who embrace His truth and His grace, and who will get with His agenda!**

Hey Paul says, *"...**preaching the gospel all the way!**"*

That means this gospel is going to take you beyond your comfort zone!

Ha... ha... ha...

Hallelujah!

This gospel is going to take you into the greatest adventure with Jesus you have ever known; *the greatest adventure you can ever have imagined!*

Ha... ha... ha...

And to you students who are already part of some school, or even if you are one of our disciples even, **listen, don't limit your adventure to an outreach team or to being part of a discipleship team, or a ministry team. You can have the greatest adventure** *every day, even right there in your own neighborhood, or in any job situation,* **when you truly discover the measure of God;** *the measure of His approval of your life, and the lives of all those around you!*

You don't need a preaching opportunity or a pulpit to be fulfilled! You don't need ministry as a crutch to bolster your identity of who you are in God's eyes! _You can enjoy life_ **and** *experience fulfillment in your Daddy's love,* **no matter what religious environment in the world you find yourself surrounded by, or what worldly environment you find yourself in!**

No matter where you are, opportunities are everywhere! Opportunities to make friends with people, and to enlighten them in the truth of gospel, *so as to impact them with the love of God!* Opportunities really are everywhere, all around you! It is all in your perspective!

Are you engaged in throne room thoughts? Are you fully engaged and enjoying your Daddy's love? Are you seeing from His perspective?

Or are you still listening and submitting to a bunch of religious nonsense?

Are you listening to the real grace message? Are you caught up in the truth of the Gospel, in your Daddy's love and embrace? Do you love people, seeing their real value because of the gospel, seeing them the way Jesus sees them?

Or are you still listening and submitting to a bunch of religious nonsense?

It makes all the difference in the world what you are submitting yourself to, and listening to, *and entertaining in your mind; in your thought-life!*

Alright, let's get to verse 15,

"We do not boast beyond measure, in other people's labors!"

112

Who are these other men, these other people Paul is referring to here? I suggest to you that they are the same prideful stubborn religious bunch Paul was referring to in verse 12, when he said,

"They are measuring themselves by themselves, and while they are measuring themselves by themselves and one another, and against us, and against one another, they are without understanding!"

Did Paul measure himself in competition to Apollos, or Cefas, meaning Peter? **No way!**

You can read there for yourself in Acts Chapter 18 there, the last portion of it, and in Acts Chapter 19 there, *how when Paul's disciples bumped into some of Apollos' disciples,* they didn't say,

'Now listen guys; Apollos, your leader, only knows as far as John the Baptist, ***and that is why you might as well leave him and come join our crew.'***

No, they didn't do that! They didn't say,

'You guys only know as far as baptism and you place too big an emphasis on an outward sign of an inward reality. You guys are good Baptists, but we are from among the more enlightened Pentecostals, you see, so let's just, you know, define our boundary lines quickly here in Antioch. Because you know, it really is a good idea, in order to promote

working together some, and to maintain at least some peace and good will among us all. Because, I mean we must make room for the Baptists and then we must also make room for the Pentecostals, because, you know, some people like it loud and other people like it a little more mellow; a little more reserved, a little more subdued and peaceful'

No man, what were Paul's disciples doing? You can go read it there in Acts, it says, and I paraphrase,

*"**They encouraged them (the disciples of Apollos they bumped into from time to time)! They edified them, and they helped to further enlighten them to fully understand the full implication of the cross, beyond John the Baptist and his message, without belittling John or these disciples they were talking to, and especially not belittling Apollos, their leader, because Paul's disciples knew they were eventually going to run into Apollos himself and they didn't want to wound or offend him before ever even getting a chance to befriend him. When they finally met with Apollos, they were able to connect in love, and help him too!**"*

They encouraged those disciples of Apollos, and then they ended up encouraging Apollos too, *because there were no competition and one-up-man-ship in their hearts!* **Their hearts were pure, and**

they had nothing but love *for Apollos and for everyone else for that matter!*

The love of God makes no room for any competition, <u>any prejudice whatsoever</u> in our hearts!

Listen, they didn't allow fleshly dogmatic *pride* to bring division, or increase any enmity and division and separation already in existence!

They didn't allow their doctrines and definitions *to become bigger than* **the love of God burning in their hearts!**

They didn't allow any doctrine or definition, no matter how good it is, to become *yet another barrier or stumbling block <u>to real love and to reveal revelation of the Father's heart</u> breaking through in their brother's hearts!*

Paul and Apollos became friends. They labored together, *even though they didn't always labor side by side.*

...And their disciples together became a powerful team *that mightily impacted the whole known world at the time!*

They all became a close knit team, *even though they didn't always labor side by side, or even operate under the same banner in registration terms of the word; in terms of their 501c3 ministry name, **because God doesn't recognize those ministry names anyway,***

He only sees one big happy family; we are all His kids anyway, as far as He is concerned, and so, they may not all have been a part of the same ministry, functioning under that same ministry name or banner, **but they recognized each other as brothers and sisters, and they recognized the fact that we have all but one Father, and so <u>instead of embracing walls and divisions</u>, they all functioned under the same banner of love; the same banner of Jesus' kingship, and under the banner of grace; the banner of the truth of the gospel!**

When Priscilla and Aquila heard that Apollos was going to Corinth, they already knew, the sparks are about to fly, because, *'Oh my, Paul has already preached in Corinth and now Apollos is going to come in there and maybe come with some weird and wonderful doctrines. And he's maybe going to confuse the brethren, and we don't know if it's such a good thing; and blah… blah… blah…'*

No! That was not their mentality! Do you know what they did? *They wrote a letter.* They, Priscilla and Aquila, Paul's companions and disciples, *wrote a letter to the saints in Corinth,* **encouraging them to receive Apollos as they would receive Paul,** *because they took the time and went out of their way to deliberately intentionally befriend Apollos, and no,* **not with a hidden agenda either,** *but with a heart full of love and encouragement, and they ended up helping*

116

him see the gospel more clearly. **They had great confidence promoting Apollos' ministry,** <u>**because they knew Apollos had now not only embraced the same revelation as Paul,**</u> **but he had embraced them all in his heart as friends now too.**

And listen, even if Apollos could get a little flaky and say something that wasn't quite enlightened, and didn't quite line up with New Testament ministry, they, Priscilla and Aquila weren't worried, or bothered by it at all, because they had enough confidence in God and in the foundation that Paul had laid down in the revelation, to not be threatened by anything coming in that might try to dislodge what Paul had established in people's hearts, so much so that, as I said, even if perhaps Apollos would preach something controversial, *they knew the saints would have* **enough maturity in love, and understanding in the truth of the gospel; enough of an intimate relationship and fellowship with God, their Daddy, in the truth of the gospel,** *to discern correctly for themselves, and sort it out for themselves.*

I say again: *They had confidence that the saints would have* **enough maturity in the love, which the revelation produced in them,** *to overlook Apollos' newness and inexperience in the revelation,* **and to not start an argument with him, or reject him, and offend and wound him.**

Priscilla and Aquila had confidence enough in the saints <u>to exhibit enough maturity in love</u> to receive from Apollos what they could agree on <u>and to let love cover the rest</u>!

Hallelujah!

How is that for ministry etiquette and church politics? *The one esteeming the other!* **The mature esteeming and serving the younger,** *overlooking their newness and inexperience in the revelation.* **Not the lesser;** *merely just the younger…*

Ha… ha… ha…

Esteeming and giving them respect! Esteeming and respecting one another!

Now that is New Testament!

Ha… ha… ha…!

We are family!

We have but one Father, amen!

And watch out, you young whipper-snappers out there, preaching the word of His grace, don't you dare get puffed up in pride, *because some of the people you may encounter, as well as other ministers you may run into, might not be more mature in the understanding of the message than you,* **but they may already be more mature in love than you.** **They may**

118

already have a more mature outlook on things! *They may already have a more mature attitude and expression developed in love, which in the end, is the accurate expression of the very life of the message you claim to know!*

Ha... ha... ha...!

I say again: **We have but one Father! We are all part of the same family!**

Walking in, and maintaining, the unity in the Spirit, in that mature bond of love and peace, *which the revelation enhances so beautifully and accurately in us, is exactly what the New testament is all about!* **That's what the gospel of grace is all about!**

Listen, *you have not grasped what this message is all about,* as long as the grace of God is still just another **doctrine** to you!

God has called us to communicate His overwhelming love to people; *not just a new doctrine!*

He has called us to impart that love, to such a degree *that it enlightens them!*

God's truth wrapped up in love *liberates!*

The truth spoken outside of love *only leads to legalistic, religious bondage,* I don't care what revelation you claim to have; or even if you preach the grace message!

If it is not the truth of His love and the demonstration of that love in delivering us and redeeming and restoring us back to our original design, that we communicate and impart to people, *then I am telling you now, we are not communicating anything worth sharing or listening to!*

You see, I want us to see clearly there, that when Paul arrived later on, he writes again to the Corinthian Church, there in 1 Corinthians 3,

He says, *'Now listen, don't you dare get petty and childish!'*

He says, *'Who died for you? Paul? Or Apollos? Peter perhaps?'*

'No!' he says, *'None of us did!'*

He says, *'We're messengers. That's all! So, don't say, 'I'm of Paul,' or 'I'm of Apollos.''*

He says, *'One sowed the seed, and the other watered. That's all we did; nothing more!'*

'It's God that gives the revelation; it's God that gives the understanding. Man, it's God alone that gives the growth; that brings the increase; not us!'

'We can pull at your leaves and try and get you to grow, but we'll never get that done! What I can do is: I can water you, I can

inspire your roots, I can inspire those roots to become established in righteousness,

...and God will get the glory as you grow, amen! Because I have nothing to do with that; that is between you and God!

I can inspire you to become established in righteousness, but God at work in you, and you yielding to Him is what brings the growth, amen!'

And so we see how Paul ministered far beyond the limits of religious church politics!

He says in 2 Corinthians 10:15,

"We are not boasting in other people's labors!"

"I praise God for every other man, every other person, who labors amongst you!"

Before we finish up in 2 Corinthians 10, I must read this in 1 Corinthians 15 to you as well.

Look at this; he says, verse 10,

"By the grace of God I am what I am!"

"...and His grace towards me was not in vain!"

He says, *"On the contrary, I worked harder than any of them!"*

Why?

"...because of the inspiration of grace!"

"...because of that love quickened within me!"

He says, *"...yet it wasn't really I in myself, it was the grace of God which was with me!"*

You see, when grace inspires you, *you can no longer limit your activities to a program!*

Verse 11 says,

"Whether then it was I or they, so we all preached, and you believed!"

Don't get snared into, *'Oh, I can't decide, I'm not sure now who impacted and influenced my life more? ...so I can say, I'm of Paul, or I'm of Apollos?'*

Listen, the thing is not whether you're of Paul, or whether you're of Apollos; the thing is *whether you are of God or not; the thing is whether you believed or not!*

You were preached to and taught, *and you believed, and that's what counts!*

Now let's go back to 2 Corinthians 10:15, and we'll close there! In the second part of Verse 15 Paul says,

"Our hope is..."

122

When Paul speaks of his hope, **he speaks of his vision for his ministry and for the Church as a whole;** **he is talking about his future anticipation for us all!**

He says,

"Our hope is that as your understanding increases; as your faith increases, our field among you may be greatly enlarged!"

God told me personally,

'Rudi, that's the only strategy that I have for you and your ministry and for my Church as a whole!'

'My hope, My faith-expectation is that as your understanding increases; as your faith increases, My field among you may be greatly enlarged!"

If any of us settle for a lesser measure of our lives and our ministries, **a lesser strategy than clarifying the gospel, we will miss God!**

My total focus in ministry is to see your understanding increase, *to see your faith increase! I want to see your faith increase!*

...Not faith for better things, to kind of help you in your process of survival, but a faith that would accurately discern what was revealed and accomplished by God our Father, in Jesus Christ!

I want you to have a faith that would accurately appreciate and appropriate the full benefit of the gospel, the full benefit of the truth of redemption! So that that word; that faith of God, that accurate revelation of redemption, will mix together with your faith, *and inspire a new action, a new activity, a new energy resource within you!*

...So that God's sphere of influence and impact among you and within you, and also out from you, may be greatly enlarged!

In Proverbs 4 you can go study and see *how it speaks about the springs of life that spring forth as a result of the abiding word.*

That is exactly what God has in mind with the truth of redemption, **and with your understanding and embrace and treasuring of that truth.**

He wants to so release a fountain of living water within you, that you will live an adventurous life, *motivated by His love*; *a life beyond your own personal needs!* **And instead, you begin to see your neighbor's need, not just some physical, soulish need (that too),** *but their need for the same revelation in the truth of the gospel; for the same love and life you enjoy!*

That is what motivated the apostles and the early Church, **and that is what motivates me today to share the gospel with people, and to also challenge you like this,** *so that* *rivers of living water will begin to gush out of your innermost being towards your neighbor, in terms of who Jesus says your neighbor is!*

...So that our field amongst you may be greatly enlarged; *may be greatly multiplied!*

...Far beyond any kind of church roster, you know, a church membership list; beyond any kind of computer list of names!

Greatly enlarged!

Greatly multiplied!

Because verse 16 says,

"...to reach those, even in countries beyond your own!"

God sees *a great multiplication* through the revelation of His grace in your life!

There are people and places you will touch and reach that I will never even meet, and rightly so! We live in a big big world and there is no way just a few of us can reach them all! No, it is going to take all of us, it is going to take the whole body of Christ energized and mobilized by the very love and passion and zeal of God Himself to do this! The world is ignorant and blind to the truth and love and faith of God, and in full on self-destruct mode, because of it, and

God wants to use <u>us</u> to turn this world around, *but it is going to take all of us!*

Father, thank you for the revelation of this mystery!

Father, we are not of those who shrink back, but we will present ourselves to You, *our very bodies a living sacrifice.*

Father, would You accelerate **Your vision within us, for the ministry You have in mind for all of us.** Not only for me and for us in our ministry, **but for Your Church as a whole?!**

Would you accelerate that vision Father, through every individual who is a part of Your Church, and especially through every person who has read this book and this series and grasped the revelation in it?!

Would You accelerate Your strategy for their lives, Father?!

Father, would You accelerate Your strategy for the New Testament Church of the Lord Jesus Christ in this country of ours, the United States of America, and in every other nation on the face of the earth f*ar beyond the boundaries of this land,* **as You inspire an obedience of <u>faith</u> within us all?!**

In Jesus Name

Amen

In closing, I urge you to get yourself a copy of the Mirror Study Bible; *it is the best paraphrased translation of the Scriptures from the original Greek that I have ever read,* **because it reveals all the nuances even, of God's heart and of Paul's gospel, the clearest.** It's available online at Barnes & Noble and several other book sellers.

If you want me or someone from of our team to come to where you are, *anywhere in the world,* and give a talk, or teach you and some of your friends *about the gospel message and these redemption realities,* simply contact us at www.LivingWordIntl.com, or you can always find me on Facebook.

If your life has changed as a result of reading this book, *please write to me and let me know.*

I would love to share in your joy *so that my joy in writing this book may be full!*

That which was from the
beginning,

which we have heard
(with our spiritual ears),
which we have seen
(with our spiritual eyes),
which we have looked upon
**(beheld, focused our attention
upon)**,
and which our hands have also
handled
**(which we have also
experienced)**,

concerning the Word of life,

we declare to you,

that you also may have this
fellowship with us;

and truly our fellowship is with
the Father
and with His Son Jesus Christ.

And these things we write to you
that your joy may be full.

~ 1John 1:1-4

130

About the Author

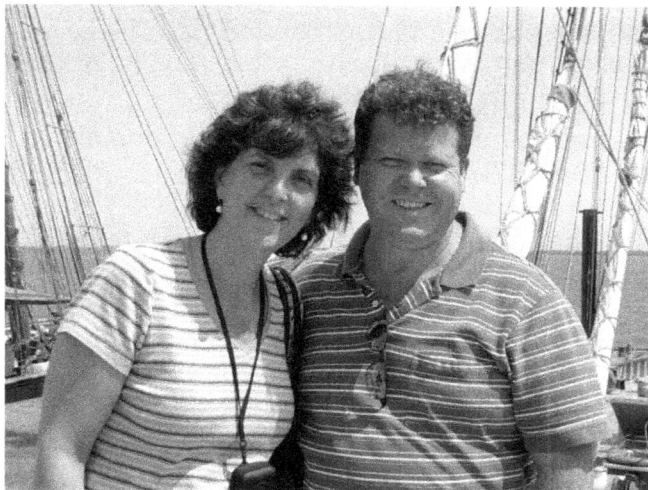

Rudi & Carmen Louw named their ministry: Living Word International.

They love to travel and minister both locally and internationally.

Rudi was born and raised in the country of South Africa, while Carmen grew up in Cortland, New York.

They function in the ministry of reconciliation (2 Corinthians 5:18-21) and flow strongly with the Holy Spirit and His anointing to teach, preach, prophesy, heal, and whatever is needed **to touch people's lives with the reality of God's love and power.**

God has given them keen insight into what He has to say to Mankind in the work of redemption concerning the revelation and restoration of humanity's true identity.

Therefore they emphasize THE GOSPEL, IN CHRIST REALITIES, the GRACE of God, the WORD OF RIGHTEOUSNESS, *and all such eternal truths essential to salvation and living the CHRIST-LIFE.*

They have been granted this wisdom and revelation into the knowledge of God by the resurrected Spirit of Jesus Christ, *to establish and strengthen believers in the faith of God, and to activate them in ministering to others.*

Not only are people set free from the poison and bondage of sin, condemnation and all kinds of intimidation, (upheld, strengthened and reinforced by age old religious ideas born out of ignorance) **but many are brought into a closer more intimate relationship with Father God, as Daddy**, through accurate teaching and unveiling of the gospel message, prophetic words, healings and miracles.

Rudi & Carmen are closely knitted together with many other effective Christians, Church fellowships, and groups of believers who share the same revelation and passion *to impart the truth of the gospel to others, **and so to impact and transform the world we live in with the LOVE and POWER of God.***